How the Bible Begins

How the Bible Begins

A Sociological Study

John R. Heapes

RESOURCE *Publications* • Eugene, Oregon

HOW THE BIBLE BEGINS
A Sociological Study

Copyright © 2021 John R. Heapes. All rights reserved. Except for brief quotations in critical publications or reviews, no part of this book may be reproduced in any manner without prior written permission from the publisher. Write: Permissions, Wipf and Stock Publishers, 199 W. 8th Ave., Suite 3, Eugene, OR 97401.

Resource Publications
An Imprint of Wipf and Stock Publishers
199 W. 8th Ave., Suite 3
Eugene, OR 97401

www.wipfandstock.com

PAPERBACK ISBN: 978-1-7252-9690-9
HARDCOVER ISBN: 978-1-7252-9689-3
EBOOK ISBN: 978-1-7252-9691-6

05/20/21

Scripture quotations taken from the (NASB®) New American Standard Bible®, Copyright © 1960, 1971, 1977, 1995, 2020 by The Lockman Foundation. Used by permission. All rights reserved. www.lockman.org

Scripture quotations taken from the Amplified® Bible (AMPC), Copyright © 1954, 1958, 1962, 1964, 1965, 1987 by The Lockman Foundation. Used by permission. www.lockman.org

To my religious and lay teachers at St. Francis Xavier School and Parish, Monsignor Scanlan High School (formerly St. Helena), and Iona College

Contents

List of Tables, Maps, and Figures | ix
Preface | xiii
Acknowledgment | xvii
Introduction | xix

Part I: The Bible's Structure | 1
Chapter 1: The Architecture of the Bible | 3

Part II: Sociology | 17
Chapter 2: What is Sociology? | 19

Part III: First Five Books of the Bible | 31
Chapter 3: Genesis | 33
Chapter 4: Exodus | 60
Chapter 5: Leviticus | 79
Chapter 6: Numbers | 89
Chapter 7: Deuteronomy | 106

Part IV: Commentary on the First Five Books of the Bible | 117
Chapter 8: Observations on the Torah/Pentateuch | 119

Part V: Sociological Analysis | 131
Chapter 9: A Dramaturgical Analysis of the Torah/Pentateuch | 133

Part VI: Conclusion | 157
Chapter 10: Finale | 159

Appendix A: Biblical Genealogy | 165
Appendix B: World History in Biblical Times and Biblical Relationships | 167
Bibliography | 177

List of Tables, Maps, and Figures

Table 1.1: Old Testament | 4

Table 1.2: New Testament | 6

Table 1.3: Bible book authors (based on tradition) | 7

Table 1.4: Year Bible books written | 9

Map 1.1: Garden of Eden | 11

Map 1.2: Mt. Ararat—Noah's Ark landing site | 12

Map 1.3: Promised Land | 13

Map 3.1: Tigris and Euphrates Rivers with Garden of Eden | 49

Map 3.2: Mt. Ararat in Turkey | 50

Map 3.3: Land of Shinar and Tower of Babel | 51

Map 3.4: Canaan, Abraham's journey, and the Chaldeans | 52

Map 3.5: Gomorrah, Sodom, Moabites, and Ammonites | 53

Map 3.6: Jacob's route from Beersheba to Haran and his return from Paddan-aram to Canaan (Israel) | 54

Map 3.7: Canaan (Israel) and Egypt | 55

Map 3.8: Location of the Genesis story on a modern-day map | 56

Map 4.1: Land occupied by Canaanites, Amorites, Hittites, Perizzites, Hivites, and Jebusites | 68

Map 4.2: Significant Egyptian sites | 74

List of Tables, Maps, and Figures

Map 4.3: Mt. Sinai (Horeb); the Wildernesses of Shur, Sinai, and Sin; and Reuel (Edom) | 75

Map 4.4: Israelites' Exodus from Egypt to the doorstep of Canaan | 76

Map 5.1: Two locations of Mt. Sinai: Egypt and Midian | 86

Map 6.1: Seven of the ethnic groups | 98

Map 6.2: Journey (blue arrows) through the wilderness and land markings | 101

Map 6.3: Promised Land boundaries according to Genesis | 102

Map 6.4: Promised Land boundaries according to Numbers | 103

Map 7.1: Tribes inside and outside (Reuben, Gad, and half of Manasseh) the Promised Land—Twelve Tribes of Israel | 111

Map 7.2: From Mt. Sinai to Mt. Nebo—Moses' last journey | 114

Figure 2.1: Diagram of Social Situations | 21

Figure 2.2: Foundation for the Diagram of Social Situations | 23

Figure 2.3: Diagram of Social Situations with foundation | 23

Figure 2.4: Diagram of Social Situations with norms | 24

Figure 3.1: Noah's sons from Adam's descendants | 34

Figure 3.2: Shem's lineage to Abram/Abraham | 35

Figure 3.3: Isaac and Ismael's father and mothers | 37

Figure 3.4: Genesis genealogy from Adam to Noah and his sons | 41

Figure 3.5: Genealogy from Shem through Abraham to Joseph and Ephraim | 42

Figure 3.6: Tracing generations from Adam to Joseph | 47

Figure 3.7: Notable people in Genesis | 48

Figure 3.8: Timeline of people and events in Figure 3.7 | 48

Figure 4.1: Moses' ancestors | 61

List of Tables, Maps, and Figures

Figure 4.2: Court of the Tabernacle | 67

Figure 4.3: Ark of the Covenant | 67

Figure 6.1: Twelve Tribes of Israel with their populations | 90

Figure 8.1: The first five books of the Bible | 119

Figure 8.2: Individuals named in the first five Bible books | 120

Figure 8.3: Genesis characters and events | 123

Figure 9.1: Diagram of Social Situations applied to the Garden of Eden | 136

Figure 9.2: Ten Commandments incorporated into the Diagram of Social Situations | 141

Figure 9.3: God as socializing agent | 144

Figure 9.4: God's diagram for humans eating fish | 146

Figure 9.5: God's diagram for humans eating locusts | 146

Figure 10.1: Torah/Pentateuch chapter and verses | 159

Figure 10.2: Summary of the first five Bible books | 161

Figure A.1: Biblical genealogy from 4004 BCE to 30 AD | 166

Figure B.1: From Adam to Moses—Dates | 169

Figure B.2: Genesis 4 and 5 Genealogy—Adam and Eve to Shem | 171

Figure B.3: Genesis 10–11, 16, 19, 21–22, 24–25, 28–30, 34–35 Genealogy—Noah's descendants | 173

Figure B.3.1: Genesis 35–36, 38, 41, and 50 genealogy—Noah's descendants (*Figure B.3.1 is a continuation of Figure B.3.*) | 174

Figure B.4: Abraham's sons and grandsons | 175

Preface

THIS BOOK'S IDEA CAME from my previous work, *Other Worlds: UFOs, Aliens, and the Afterlife*. This book described aliens living in other worlds in space and the deceased occupying another world in time. Aliens and the dead dwelled in worlds other than our own.

How is the Bible an example of another world? This book visualizes the Bible as a gestalt, that is, as a configuration constituted as a functional whole—a world unto itself. It is a realm distinguished from the one in which we inhabit. Hence, the Bible is not portrayed literally as another world, but only conceptually as one. I assert that biblical content constitutes another world.

In a secular age, the Bible is not a popular area of study. Although Google listed scores of studies of this profoundly popular book, sociology has not done much recently. Ferdinand Schureman Schenck wrote *Sociology of the Bible*, a questionable sociological, review over a century ago.

Schenck's approach identified how God's plan for humans could make for a better world, as I understand it. The problem with Schenck's method, however, is that it is *not* sociology. He *prescribed* how one must live; sociology *describes* how people live, not how they *should* live. Sociology analyzes how social factors, such as race and class, affect people's behavior. Additionally, Schenck's 1909 book is outdated.

Some more recently published social science / sociology-oriented books on the Bible include: Jonathan S. Greer, John W.

Preface

Hilber, and John H. Walton, eds., *Behind the Scenes of the Old Testament: Cultural, Social, and Historical Contexts*; Richard L. Rohrbaugh, ed., *Social Science and New Testament Interpretation*; and Anthony J. Blasi, *Social Science and the Christian Scriptures, 3-volume set: Sociological Introductions and New Translation.*

Although these books have a social science / sociology approach, they neither concentrate on the first five books of the Bible nor apply a dramaturgical method to study their content. Greer's book employed dramaturgical language to organize its content table, but he did not use this approach to analyze book content. Most publications using a social science / sociology style feature the New Testament and not the first five Bible books. We need a genuine sociological study of a book with a readership more significant than any other published.

Our purpose is not to prove or disprove the validity of biblical content or its message. For instance, some believers claim that God created the Earth in approximately 4000 BCE. Scientists, however, establish Earth's birth as about 4.5 billion years ago. The text of this book does not take sides on this issue. The approach merely identifies sociological content, such as occupations found in Genesis.

People need to be cautious in reading this book. First, I am not a biblical scholar, and many may not agree with my interpretations of biblical verses. Biblical scholars have written scores of books and produced a plethora of websites explaining biblical content. I encourage readers to retrieve these sources to understand God's message to humanity. Second, this is not a sociological study that tests hypotheses. Instead, it is an exploratory study that comes before social scientists formulate and test their hypotheses.

This volume focuses on the first five books of the Bible: Genesis, Exodus, Leviticus, Numbers, and Deuteronomy. Together, these books form the Torah for the Jewish faith and the Pentateuch for Christians.

As a sociologist, I am qualified to apply the sociological perspective to study the Bible. I have taught this discipline for over forty years, and have spent hours reading and re-reading the first five books of the Bible.

Preface

The sociological viewpoint may enhance believers' understanding of the book they consider a sacred text. It may intrigue non-believers and help them understand how this well-read text is an exceptional piece of writing. In either case, this sociological study will show who populates the religious text, what rules (norms) govern their lives, and what social problems they dealt with, as well as many other aspects of their social lives.

Acknowledgment

My sincere thanks to my wife, Sheila. She grounded me throughout this project and my life.

Introduction

How Was a Version Of the Bible Selected For Study?

AT FIRST, THE NUMBER of biblical versions confounded me. Which one should I use? Then, I misunderstood what "version" meant. At first, I thought each was a different Bible. Later I realized version meant a translation of the Bible. Diverse groups of scholars have translated the Bible into English (or another native tongue, such as French), and each group gave their version a specific name. For example, the King James Version (KJV), published in 1611, served as *the* Bible for 300 years.[1] Now, among others, there is the New International Version (NIV), published in 1978; the New American Standard Bible (NASB), issued in 1995; and the New American Bible (NAB), released in 2011.

Moreover, these versions fall into two categories: (1) faithfulness to form and (2) commitment to meaning. Some Bibles are word-by-word translations or a formal equivalence. For instance, if a phrase in the original Hebrew Bible had twelve words, scholars transcribed these exact words into English, word-for-word. The second category of translators (i.e., dynamic/functional equivalence) sought to capture a phrase's meaning correctly. They pursued a phrase-for-phrase translation of the Bible.[2]

---

1. Ward, "5 Guidelines."
2. Wallace, "Choosing a Bible Translation."

Introduction

Some have estimated there are more than fifty versions of the Bible written in English.[3] I decided to select the U.S. Bible version meeting these criteria: most popular, best-selling, most accurate according to scholars, and most comfortable to read for beginners. Two American Bible versions met these criteria: NIV and NASB.[4]

Additionally, NIV balances the word-for-word and phrase-for-phrase bible types, and by using contemporary grammatical forms, its Bible is easier to understand. NASB follows the style of KJV, but it uses modern English instead of the archaic terminology found in KJV.[5] English-speaking countries have used the KJV for 300 years, so it was necessary to include NASB, its "cousin," in this study.

The NASB version forms the basis of study in this book. Many Protestant churches use it. Occasionally, I used the Amplified Bible because it incorporates plain-speaking English.

How Is the Bible Studied Sociologically?

Sociology is the study of human interaction. It examines, for instance, how people's religious ideas influence their behavior with others, such as how people who believe in the sanctity of life vote to legalize abortion or go to war.

Sociological concepts make up the sociological perspective. For example, "sanctions" are rewards or punishments; "socializing agents" are people or things instructing individuals how to behave. When individuals metaphorically look through sociological concepts, they see the social context shaping people's behavior. It is as if they see invisible marks on a floor into which people step, and they act accordingly. Such as, when a professor (socializing agent) walks into a classroom to teach students (socializees) how to dissect a frog, this instructor engages in a socialization process. Teachers may give early dismissal to students who follow directions (positive sanctions).

3. Interactive Bible, "Different Versions of the Bible?"
4. Filipovski, "Bible Translations."
5. Cambridge University Press, "Bibles."

Introduction

So, sociological questions about the Bible include: What rules (norms) guide biblical characters' behavior? What social statuses (e.g., occupations) do biblical people hold? What is the sexual identities of biblical figures? Are there more males or females depicted in the Bible?

Because a sociological discussion of the Bible does not delve into the religious any conclusions should be academic.

PART I

The Bible's Structure

CHAPTER 1

The Architecture of the Bible

THE BIBLE HAS BEEN described as the "greatest book ever written." Its readership is the largest of any book with an estimated 3.9 billion copies sold worldwide.[1] Why have so many people bought this book? The following five questions attempt to get an answer.

1. What is the Bible?

"Bible" literally means "book." The Bible is a compilation of books split into two parts: Old and New testaments. There are thirty-nine books in the Protestant Old Testament, while the Catholic version has forty-six books. Protestant and Catholic versions of the New Testament have twenty-seven books. (See Tables 1.1 and 1.2. Italicized names are found only in the Catholic Bible.)

---

1. Reference.com, "How Many Copies of the Bible Have Been Sold?"

Part I: The Bible's Structure

Table 1.1: Old Testament

Protestant Version	Catholic Version	Protestant Version	Catholic Version
Genesis	Genesis	Job	*Judith*
Exodus	Exodus	Psalms	Esther
Leviticus	Leviticus	Proverbs	*1st Maccabees*
Numbers	Numbers	Ecclesiastes	*2nd Maccabees*
Deuteronomy	Deuteronomy	Song Of Songs	Job
Joshua	Joshua	Isaiah	Psalms
Judges	Judges	Jeremiah	Proverbs
Ruth	Ruth	Lamentations	Ecclesiastes
1st Samuel	1st Samuel	Ezekiel	Song Of Songs
2nd Samuel	2nd Samuel	Daniel	*Wisdom*
1st Kings	1st Kings	Hosea	*Ecclesiasticus/ Sirach*
2nd Kings	2nd Kings	Joel	Isaiah
1st Chronicles	1st Chronicles	Amos	Jeremiah
2nd Chronicles	2nd Chronicles	Obadiah	Lamentations
Ezra	Ezra	Jonah	*Baruch*
Nehemiah	Nehemiah	Micah	Ezekiel
Esther	*Tobit*	Nahum	Daniel

The Architecture of the Bible

Protestant Version	Catholic Version
Habakkuk	Hosea
Zephaniah	Joel
Haggai	Amos
Zechariah	Obadiah
Malachi	Jonah
	Micah
	Nahum
	Habakkuk
	Zepphaniah
	Haggai
	Zechariah
	Malachi

Part I: The Bible's Structure

Table 1.2: New Testament

Protestant and Catholic Versions	Protestant and Catholic Versions
Matthew	1st Timothy
Mark	2nd Timothy
Luke	Titus
John	Philemon
Acts	Hebrews
Romans	James
1st Corinthians	1st Peter
2nd Corinthians	2nd Peter
Galatians	1st John
Ephesians	2nd John
Philippians	3rd John
Colossians	Jude
1st Thessalonians	Revelation
2nd Thessalonians	

Why are there more books in the Catholic Old Testament than in the Protestant version? Protestants did not want books in their Bible that were not part of the original Hebrew Bible, which resulted in a Protestant version with sixty-six books with 1,189 chapters and 31,173 verses.[2]

2. Bible Info, "Who wrote the Bible?"

2. Who Wrote the Bible?

Forty authors have been identified for the Old and New testaments. The first author, however, was Moses.[3] He wrote the first five books of the Bible. Scholars credit Moses with writing about 20 percent of the biblical text, and as such, he is considered the most prolific biblical writer.

Biblical authors are cited in Table 1.3.[4]

Table 1.3: Bible Authors (based on tradition)

BOOK	AUTHOR
Genesis	Moses
Exodus	Moses
Leviticus	Moses
Numbers	Moses
Deuteronomy	Moses
Joshua	
Judges	
Ruth	Unknown
1st & 2nd Samuel	
1st & 2nd Kings	
1st & 2nd Chronicles	
Ezra	Ezra
Nehemiah	Nehemiah
Esther	
Job	Unknown
	Various
	David: 73
	Asaph: 12
	Sons of Korah: 11
Psalms	Solomon: 2
	Moses: 1
	Ethan: 1
	Heman: 1 (with Korah)
	Various
Proverbs	Solomon: 29
	Agur: 1
	Lemuel: 1
Ecclesiastes	Solomon
Song of Solomon	
Isaiah	Isaiah
Jeremiah	Jeremiah
Lamentations	

3. John is known as the last biblical writer.
4. Kranz, "35 Authors."

Part I: The Bible's Structure

BOOK cont.	AUTHOR cont.
Ezekiel	Ezekiel
Daniel	Daniel
Hosea	Hosea
Joel	Joel
Amos	Amos
Obadiah	Obadiah
Jonah	Jonah
Micah	Micah
Nahum	Nahum
Habakkuk	Habakkuk
Zephaniah	Zephaniah
Haggai	Haggai
Zechariah	Zechariah
Malachi	Malachi
Matthew	Matthew
Mark	Mark
Luke	Luke
John	John
Acts	Acts
Romans	
1st & 2nd Corinthians	
1st & 2nd Corinthians	
Galatians	
Ephesians	
Philippians	Paul
Colossians	
1st & 2nd Thessalonians	
1st & 2nd Timothy	
Titus	
Philemon	
Hebrews	Hebrews
James	James (brother of Jesus)
1st & 2nd Peter	Peter
1st, 2nd, & 3rd John	John
Jude	Jude
Revelation	John

Table 1.3 cites twenty-nine individuals who authored Old Testament books, along with a group, the sons of Korah. While there are only ten individuals cited as New Testament authors, groups are named, such as Hebrews and Acts. Authorship of the remainder of the Bible remains unknown.

The Architecture of the Bible

3. When Was the Bible Written?[5]

Table 1.4 cites the authorship year of biblical books.

Table 1.4: Year Bible books written

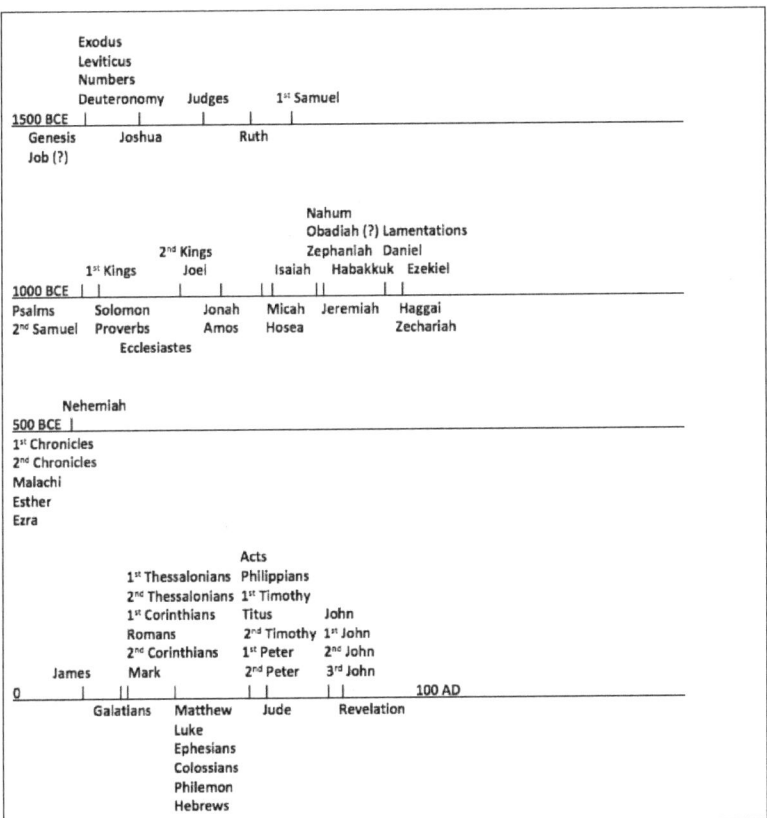

People wrote the Bible over a span of 1600 years. Around 1500 BCE, the first versions were composed, and about 100 AD, authors wrote the last sentences. This time spanned from the Vedic Age in India when Hindu sacred texts (i.e., Vedas) were composed to around the time Romans built Hadrian's Wall in Great Britain.[6]

---

5. Bible Info, "Who wrote the Bible?"
6. New World Encyclopedia, "Vedic Period."; Schulman, "Hadrian's Wall."

Part I: The Bible's Structure

However, the biblical story covers over 4,000 years of history, from approximately 4000 BCE (the time of Genesis) to 33 AD (the death of Christ). The Bible, however, does not record anything between 1804 BCE and 4 BCE. So, the most remarkable story ever told covers approximately 2,600 years of God's history of interacting with humankind.

4. Where Did Biblical Action Take Place?

The biblical story begins in Genesis with God creating the physical world and the first humans: Adam and Eve. They resided in the Garden of Eden, but where was this place?

By most accounts, Adam and Eve resided on a "fertile crescent" between the Tigris and Euphrates rivers in Mesopotamia ("place between two rivers"). These rivers run parallel from their eastern Turkey sources and flow southeast through Syria and Iraq into the Persian Gulf.

The Architecture of the Bible

Map 1.1: Garden of Eden

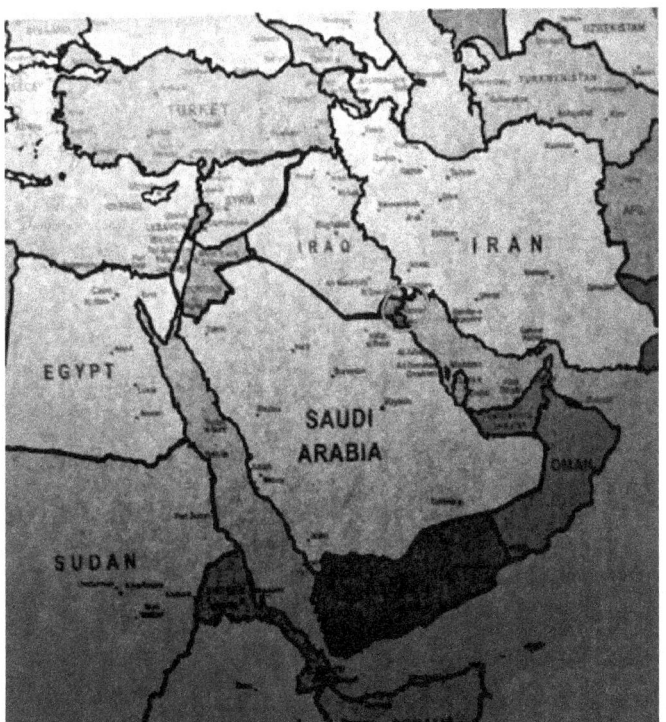

Source: Ian Macky, PAT

About 1,000 years later, Noah saved all living creatures on his Ark during the Great Flood. After forty days and forty nights of rain that submerged the earth, his boat landed on top of Mt. Ararat in Turkey. (See Map 1.2.)

Part I: The Bible's Structure

Map 1.2: Mt. Ararat—Noah's Ark landing site

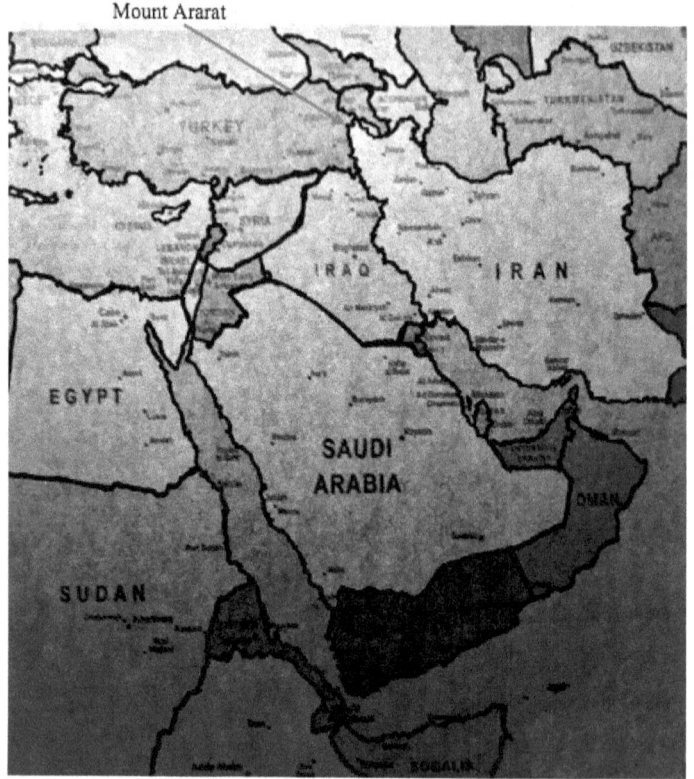

Source: Ian Macky, PAT

Another 1,000 years had passed after the flood when Abraham led his people from Mesopotamia to a land promised to them by God. This territory was Canaan, a "land of milk and honey." According to the University of Pennsylvania Museum of Archaeology and Anthropology, this place was the southern Levant, which today includes: Israel, West Bank, Gaza, Jordan, and southern parts of Syria and Lebanon. (See Map 1.3.)

Map 1.3: Promised Land

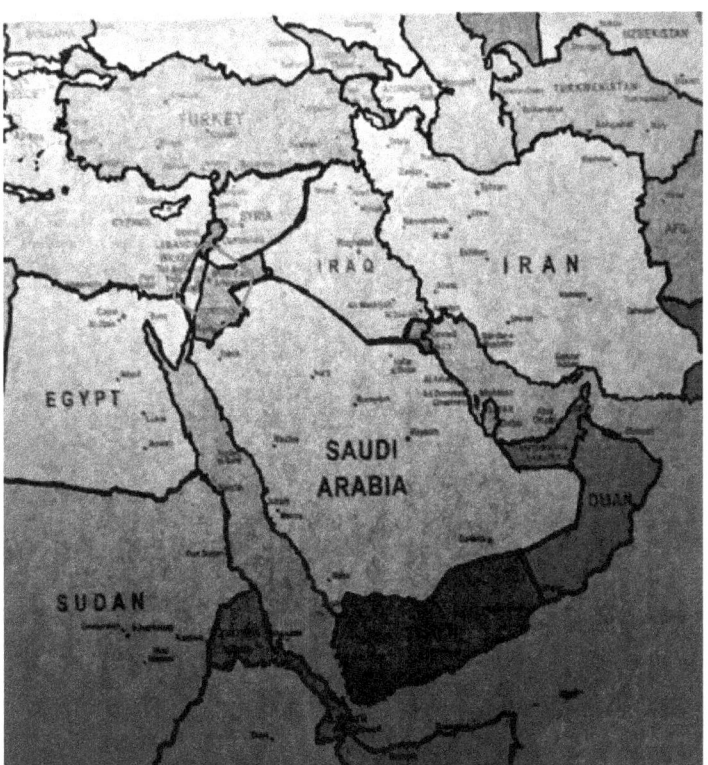

Source: Ian Macky, PAT

Abraham's descendants did not stay in Canaan (the Promised Land) because of famine; they moved to Egypt. These "Israelites" stayed in Egypt for 430 years, first as free people and then as slaves. It was not until about 1446 BCE that Moses led the Hebrews out of Egypt for the Promised Land. Moses died at the doorstep of the Promised Land, and the Torah/Pentateuch ended.

Part I: The Bible's Structure

5. Why?

Why were the first five books of the Bible (i.e., the Torah or Pentateuch) written? What was the Torah's purpose?

A summary follows of the Jewish Virtual Library's account of the evolution of the Torah's purpose.[7] This explanation runs the gamut from a sacred text originating with God to a secular work written by humans. Initially, people viewed the Torah as God's blueprint for creating the world. One author writes, ". . . God created the world by looking into the Torah as an architect builds a palace by looking into blueprints."

Another author, however, advances a rationalist theory. The Torah is understandable by using one's reasoning faculty. For instance, reason tells us that murder is wrong. Others oppose a rationalist interpretation. They hold that the commandments were exclusively from God. The Lord revealed his will to those who listened.

In the twelfth century, Maimonides, a great medieval Jewish philosopher, argued the Torah was a product of Moses' prophecy. He claimed the Torah had two purposes:

1. The body's well-being to attain the ultimate political goal of a well-functioning governance system for city and state.
2. The welfare of the soul (intellect) to achieve immortality through one's mind on the highest things.

Maimonides saw the Torah as leverage against superstition, appetite, and idolatry. Spanish kabbalists moved consideration of the Torah to a metaphysical level. They said the Torah was God, and he/it was a living organism.

Spinoza, a famous seventeenth century Jewish philosopher, said the Torah originated within man's mind and not in God's mind. Israel produced the Torah; it did not create Israel. The Torah was best understood within a historical context and recognized as primitive and unscientific.

---

7. Jewish Virtual Library, "Judaism."

Later, some scholars moved away from Spinoza's non-divine origin stance. They returned to the previous interpretation of a divine origin but fused reason into it. In other words, they saw the Torah as political law given to Israel by God. Intellectualizing the Torah, however, was opposed by Samuel Luzzatto, a famous Jewish Italian scholar in the nineteenth century. He held the starting point of Judaism as the belief that God revealed the Torah to Hebrews.

In the twentieth century, Martin Buber, a renowned German-Jewish philosopher, held the Torah was not law but rather an instruction. He recognized the Torah's purpose was to convert the universe and God from "It to Thou." In the past, the Torah was a dialog between Israel and God. Presently, the Torah has become an interchange between the reader and God. Buber instructed readers to be open to the entire Torah but heed only those parts that resonated with them.

According to the Jewish Library, today most writers maintain a secularist interpretation of the Torah. They suggest God did not reveal it, but rather it was a product of ancient Israel's national life. However, Leibowitz, an outspoken twentieth century Jewish thinker, emphasized that the Torah was a law for God's worship, and it abolished the worship of men and things.

PART II

Sociology

CHAPTER 2

What is Sociology?

Sociology: Definition

SOCIOLOGY IS THE SCIENTIFIC study of human interaction and the body of knowledge that results from such study.[1] This discipline, like others, is comprised of concepts with terms such as *norms*, *roles*, and *status*.[2] By comparison, examples of psychological concepts are personality, introversion, and attitudes.

Concepts function as a lens through which people look and, depending upon which lens they look through, they see different things. A photographer looking through a thirty-five-millimeter (mm) lens sees a landscape differently from one looking through a seventy-mm lens. A person looking through a sociological lens sees other things than a person looking through a psychological lens.

If a house stands in a field, a photographer using a seventy-mm camera will draw closer to the home than if he or she uses a thirty-five-mm camera. In a like manner, when people use psychological concepts, they examine an individual's mental or emotional workings. Sociological concepts pull back one's attention to

---

1. Adapted from Dressler, *Sociology*, 3.

2. The author italicizes sociological concepts when they first appear in the text. All other times they remain in standard form.

include the group or society within which a person behaves. For instance, if people jump up and down in a house, a psychologist may explain that their behavior results from their extroverted personalities. A sociologist seeing the same behavior may explain that these people are holding the status of "party-goer," and they play out the role of dancer. Personality is inside a person; status and role are outside of an individual. Or, where psychology examines "inside," sociology studies "outside." Likewise, psychology studies "me," while sociology analyzes "we." Which perspective is right, psychology or sociology? They are both correct. They look at a situation from different viewpoints.

The sociological perspective applied to the Bible allows us to see the social environment biblical figures occupied: in what types of societies these people live and what statuses these individuals held in these societies. A sociologically-conscious person can describe biblical cultures and the relationships among the characters that occupy these social terrains.

How is Society Structured?

Social units, such as a *society* (e.g., the United States or France) or a *group* (e.g., New Orleans Saints or New York Yankees), have structure. This edifice is invisible to those who do not have a sociological vision to see it. A diagram that makes visible a hidden structure around which social units of any size take shape is pictured in Figure 2.1. Just as a skeleton gives shape to an organism, this diagram gives shape to social units. For example, if a skeleton is eight to thirteen feet or three to four inches, it could be an elephant in the first instance or a mouse in the second case. In a like manner, social units take on a particular shape depending upon which *values* and norms constitute their structure. So, if a society values an individual, while another values a group, how these societies appear will be different. The society in the first instance may appreciate hard work, but the second may treasure the common good.

What is Sociology?

The diagram giving shape to social units I call the *Diagram of Social Situations*.[3] Situations, large and small, can be explained by this diagram. For example, a diagram shapes a society's form and sculpts interaction between two people. People do not see a diagram, but it is there. The Diagram of Social Situations is like air—it is there, but no one sees it. Only those with sociological consciousness can see a diagram present in social situations. A diagram shapes a setting and the behavior of people in that situation.

The Diagram of Social Situations looks like an American football goal post: _____|_____|_____. The horizontal line represents all possible behavior people can do in a situation. For instance, if it is lunchtime, what meat can people eat? The choices could be anything, such as beef, fish, cockroaches, or human flesh. But groups and societies do not allow their members to eat all possible meat choices. They establish certain types as appropriate for their members, while other types are deemed inappropriate. In America, eating beef, chicken, or fish for lunch is appropriate, while consuming cockroaches or human flesh is inappropriate. Appropriate lunch food for a group or society is found *inside* the two vertical lines of the goalpost, while some foodstuff is inappropriate and *outside* of these lines. Thus, a diagram takes the shape pictured in Figure 2.1.:

Figure 2.1: Diagram of Social Situations

(Inappropriate)	*(Appropriate)*	*(Inappropriate)*
Human flesh, Cockroaches	Beef, Chicken, Fish	Human flesh, Cockroaches
(A L L	P O S S I B L E	B E H A V I O R)

The following are questions and answers based on the Diagram of Social Situations.

1. What is the ultimate goal of any group or society? What must it accomplish before anything else?

   - *Answer*: Survival.

---

3. The Diagram of Social Situations does not hold every sociological concept. For example, power and social stratification are absent. However, an abbreviated version of the diagram does not diminish its clout as a summary of sociological awareness.

Part II: Sociology

2. How is survival attained? What must groups and societies do to survive?

    - *Answer*: Satisfy needs.

3. Groups and societies must meet what types of needs?

    - *Answer*: Physical and social needs.

4. What are examples of physical needs?

    - *Answer*: Needs that satisfy the body, such as food, clothing, and sex.

5. What are examples of social needs?

    - *Answer*: Needs individuals must satisfy for functioning as humans. Association with other humans is an example. If people are not in another human's presence, they will not act like a human. Why? Individuals learn how to behave from other humans. Children raised by chickens behave like chickens. They learn from those with whom they have an association.

6. How many types of physical and social needs are there?

    - *Answer*: Two—real and perceived. Actual physical needs are those humans absolutely must satisfy for survival, such as drinking water. Perceived physical needs are those humans think they need for survival but do not. For instance, many Americans believe they must "fall in love," or they will die. Falling in love is a perceived social need. Many people never "fall in love" but live happy and fulfilling lives.

        An example may be Catholic nuns who dedicate their lives to teaching children. A real social need is something humans undeniably need for their survival. As mentioned, association with other humans is necessary for survival as a human.

What is Sociology?

Figure 2.2 presents the foundation on which the Diagram of Social Situations rests.

Figure 2.2: Foundation for the Diagram of Social Situations

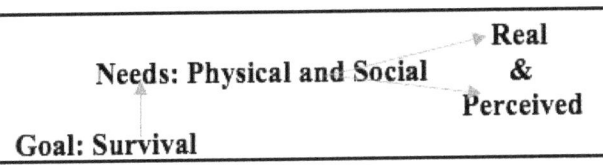

7. Do groups and societies permit their members to engage in all possible behaviors?

- *Answer*: No. Although there are multiple ways people can meet needs, groups and societies do not permit their members to engage in all of them. They select specific approaches as appropriate. Values show members these ways. For instance, on a sleepy Monday morning, an American's value to work hard and to get ahead "tells" him or her to "rise and shine." In a sense, values are like flashlights shining on preferred ways of behaving.

Based on the previous questions and answers, the Diagram of Social Situations takes on the arrangement in Figure 2.3.

Figure 2.3: Diagram of Social Situations with foundation

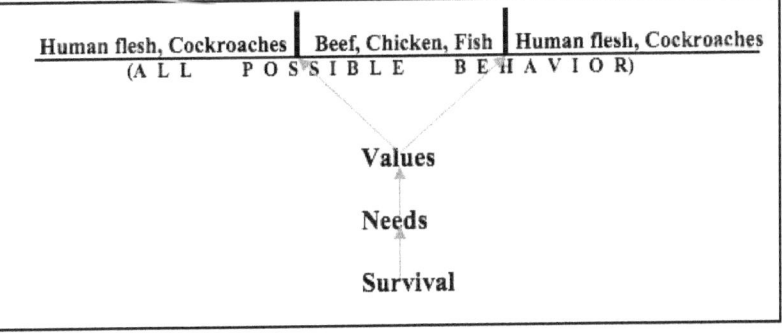

Part II: Sociology

8. Since values are subtle, as indicated by their subterranean position in Figure 2.3, how are people aware of them?

   - *Answer*: Groups and societies create norms (i.e., the diagram's vertical lines) that are rules or behavior guidelines. They distinguish, in a general way, what a social unit deems appropriate from inappropriate behavior.

Figure 2.4: Diagram of Social Situations with norms

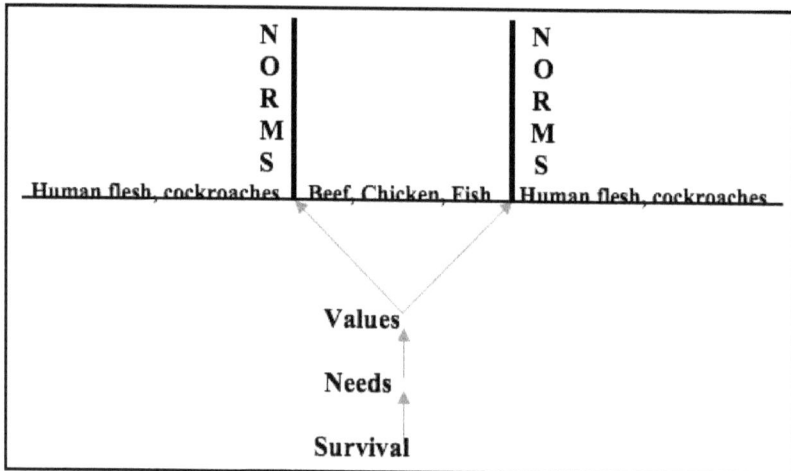

Social units use moral terms to distinguish behaviors found inside and outside of norms. Deeds found inside of norms are right, while those outside are wrong. For instance, in the United States, eating a chicken sandwich is accepted as good manners, while having a human flesh hoagie is bad manners. Norms render psychological determinations. Behaviors inside norms are normal, while behaviors outside of them are abnormal. People in American society engage in appropriate, suitable, or expected behavior when they eat fish sandwiches. Eating cockroaches is considered inappropriate, unsuitable, or abnormal.

Additionally, behavior inside norms is *normative* or *conformist*, while behavior outside of norms is *non-normative* or *deviant*. Deviants deviate from what? They diverge from their group or society's norms.

9. Do all norms have the same significance in groups and societies?

   - *Answer*: No. Depending upon how strongly a group or society wants its members to abide by them, the type of norm changes. For instance, if a group merely wishes their members to adhere to rules, these norms are *folkways*. Euphemistically, they are "baby norms." For example, rules directing us to eat peas with a fork, not a knife, are folkways. Yet another set of norms demand people to act in specific ways. A directive for marital couples to avoid affairs is an example. These are *mores*. Finally, some standards require people to behave in particular ways. These norms are *laws*. If a person kills another human, he or she has violated a law. If one broken norm receives more penalties than another, it is taken more seriously by the social unit. That is, those breaking folkways suffer lesser penalties than those breaching laws.

10. Are there situations where no norms are present?

    - *Answer*: Yes. This condition is a state of *anomie*, or normlessness. For example, when a riot breaks out at a concert, people freeze, scatter, and are in a state of general confusion because no norms guide their actions.

11. Are people born with diagrams of social situations in their heads?

    - *Answer*: No.

12. How do people acquire their group and society's diagrams?

    - *Answer*: People neither have genes with diagrams in them nor do they "pop-out" at a particular life stage. People give others diagrams through the socialization process.

Part II: Sociology

13. Who instructs in the *socialization process*?

    - *Answer*: Individuals called *socializing agents* pass along their diagrams to others. Socializing agents receive their designation, or name, from how a situation is defined. For instance, in a classroom, the socializing agent is a teacher, but this person is a drill sergeant in the army.

14. What is a novice called in a socialization process?

    - *Answer*: A *socializee*. Again, the particular designation of a socializee depends upon the social situation. In a classroom, the socializee is a student; in the army, a private.

15. How do socializing agents get socializees to behave appropriately?

    - *Answer*: Socializing agents use *positive* and *negative sanctions*. A positive sanction is a reward, such as rest and recuperation (R&R) for an army private working under a socializing agent's directives. A negative sanction is a punishment for bad behavior, as judged by the socializing agent. For instance, a student may have recess revoked for cheating on a test.

16. What do socializees receive through socialization?

    - *Answer*: Everything they need for functioning in their social world(s) is the result of socialization. Socializees learn skills, such as how to use a computer, and acquire values, such as belief in individualism.

        They also acquire statuses and roles. A status is a position a person occupies in a social situation. For instance, at 8 a.m., a person may be a mother; at 9 a.m., an office worker; and at 11 p.m. a wife. Mother, office worker, and wife are all statuses held by the same woman.

        What she does in them is called role, which is the action attached to a status. When she makes breakfast for her children, writes a report at the office, and has intimate moments with her husband, she acts out behaviors linked to her statuses as a mother, office worker, and wife. People step into statuses and act out their roles.

17. What are the results of socialization for individuals and groups?

    - *Answer*: A consequence of socialization for individuals is *social control*. So, when a child runs into a kitchen before dinner to get a cookie but stops because his mom told him not to eat pre-dinner snacks, he is socially controlled. His mother does not have to continually stand in the kitchen to prevent her son from eating cookies before dinner. Why? She is in her son's head in the form of the diagram. More broadly, the group attains *social order* through socialization. When family members run around their home with the same content on their diagrams (e.g., no snacks before dinner), social order permeates the household.

      Those who do not adopt socialization from their group or society are called deviants or non-conformists, since they are not conforming to their group or society's rules.

18. What are collective rules for societal members?

    - *Answer*: *Institutions* embody the norms (rules) of conduct focused on a particular societal need. For example, all of society's regulations governing its members' conduct in pursuit of goods and services is called the economy. Directives concentrated on the protection of society from external threats is called the military.

19. Taken together as a whole, what are the norms, statuses, and other social components of living?

    - *Answer*: *Culture* is made up of all the "things" a group of people create to survive. These "things" have material and non-material components. The material part consists of things we can see, touch, taste, and smell, such

Part II: Sociology

as computers, cars, and coffeemakers in American culture. Non-material parts of culture are a society's values, norms, institutions, among other factors.

Culture is a society's "game plan" for living. In the spirit of this book, culture is a society's Diagram of Social Situations. A society's culture, game plan, or diagram acquired through socialization shapes how its members think and act. So, if people eat beef for lunch in the United States or permit cows to roam anywhere they wish in India, it's their culture "telling" them it is appropriate, right, and/or normal. Therefore, culture, or the diagram, defines reality for people.

20. Is culture (or the diagram) fixed and static in groups and societies as well as within people's minds?

- *Answer*: Yes and no. It depends on the makeup of groups and society's stage of development. For instance, the Pennsylvania Amish have retained the same lifestyle for centuries. They do not use electricity on their farms, and they do not marry outside of their group. Most people on Earth, however, are altering their lives in significant ways.

    Social change, "the transformation of culture and social institutions over time," is vast, intense, and pervasive.[4] Transportation and technology (e.g., the internet) bring people together quickly (e.g., airplanes) who are so different that this contact can produce confusion, fear, hostility, and joy. The internet has exposed Middle Eastern cultures to Western ideas. For instance, once, women in Saudi Arabia thought they were subservient to men. Now, they consider themselves equal.

    America took about 150 years to change from an agricultural to an industrial society. Today societal transformation happens in decades with this speed having ramped up during the Industrial Age. In the current Information/Computer Age, rates of change have become

4. Macionis, *Society*, 551.

faster. At one time, parents did not understand their children, but today that has accelerated so that older siblings cannot figure out their younger counterparts.

Since those who look at the world through the Diagram of Social Situations utilize a sociological perspective, their consciousness can see the forces outside of individual's social situations that act upon them and shape their behavior.

PART III

First Five Books of the Bible

*Summaries and Understanding their Content:
Who? What? When? Where? Why? How?*

CHAPTER 3

Genesis

Who? What? When? Where? Why? How?[1]

THE FIRST FIVE BOOKS of the Bible start with the beginning of time and end with Moses' death in 1405 BCE. This epic story is told in five books: Genesis, Exodus, Leviticus, Numbers, and Deuteronomy.

Summary of the Book of Genesis

Fifty chapters and 1,515 verses comprise the book of Genesis. In Genesis 1 and 2, the author, presumed to be Moses, described the beginning of the physical world. God created light from darkness on day one, and then each day for seven days, he made everything else, including humans.

God instructs Adam and Eve, the first humans, not to eat from the tree of knowledge of good and evil. This directive is God's first norm, which Adam and Eve break. God ejects them from Paradise (i.e., negative sanction).

Later, Cain kills his brother (i.e., deviancy) because he is jealous of Abel's favorite status with God. As time passes, Adam's

1. These questions examine the demographic or population characteristics of biblical people and places.

Part III: First Five Books of the Bible

descendants engage in more evil acts. Human corruption ends with God's fury and the major flood that engulfes Earth, killing everyone except Noah and his family, who were faithful to God. (Figure 3.1 traces Noah's sons from Adam's descendants.)[2]

Figure 3.1: Noah's sons from Adam's descendants

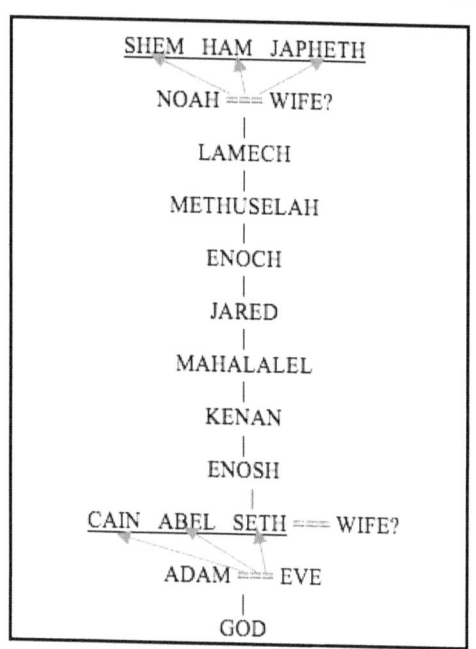

After forty days and nights of continuous rain during the Great Flood, the sun comes out and makes land dry for habitation. Then, God makes his first covenant (agreement) with humankind. The Lord promises never to destroy Earth with a flood again. He also gives man dominion over the world and its creatures.

Next, Noah and his sons (Shem, Ham, and Japheth) repopulate the world, these men's descendants dispersing throughout it. Once humans lived together and spoke a singular language. Now, God removes them from Babel, scatters, and confuses them with

---

2. Underline indicates "related people" while === denotes "married to." The figure is read from bottom to top.

many languages. The Bible traces Noah's descendants through Shem down to Abram (Abraham).[3]

Figure 3.2: Shem's lineage to Abram/Abraham (Gen 11:10–26)

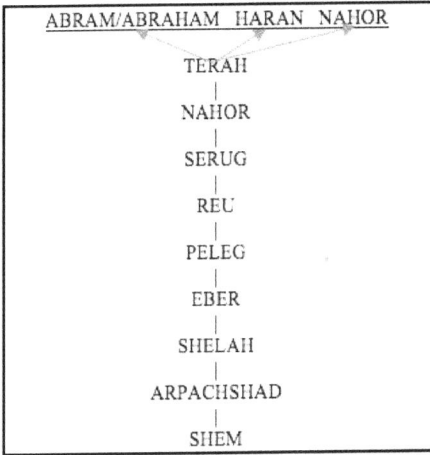

To this point, the Genesis story has covered Creation, Adam and Eve and their family, and Noah and the Flood. Thus far, this epic has covered ten generations, and then the first patriarch of the Hebrew people comes on stage.

After God chooses him and his descendants (Israelites), Abram moves them toward the Promised Land (Canaan). Since famine blighted this land, the Israelites moved to Egypt. Then the story gets complicated (Gen 3–11).

Sarai, Abram's wife, catches the attention of the Egyptian pharaoh. Abram lies to the pharaoh and claims Sarai is his sister. Consequently, the pharaoh weds her. When he learns of Abram's deception, he banishes Abram, Sarai, and Lot (Abram's nephew) from Egypt. They go to Canaan (the Promised Land). Abram and Lot's flocks are too numerous for the land, so Lot leaves and settles in the nearby Jordan Valley (Gen 12).

Next, there is a fourteen-year clash among kings. Lot is captured during one of the battles. Abram fights and wins back Lot

---

3. Haran's son was Lot. Figure 3.2 is read from bottom to top.

and his possessions but does not pilfer the defeated. So, God judges Abram righteous and promises (creates a covenant to provide) him a son and land from Egypt to the Euphrates River (Canaan) (Gen 13–14).

Sarai was barren, so she gives her maid Hagar to Abram. When Hagar and Abram conceive Ishmael, Sarai becomes jealous. Hagar leaves, but an angel tells her to return. The Lord asks Abram to enter a covenant with him and receive offspring. At this time, Abram is ninety-nine years old; Sarai is ninety. Sarai laughs when she hears God's pledge, but Abram agrees. To mark the occasion, God instructs Abram to circumcise every male under his care. God changes Abram's name to Abraham—father of many nations—and Sarai's name to Sarah—mother of nations (Gen 15–17).

The story then moves to the infamous cities of Sodom and Gomorrah. Three men (angels) appear to Abraham and threaten to destroy Sodom because of its wicked ways. Abraham bargains with them to avert catastrophe (Gen 18).

Lot lives in Sodom and hosts these men at his home. One night, Sodomite men approach Lot and request sexual relations with Lot's guests. Lot refuses, instead offering his virgin daughters. Belligerently, these Sodomites try to break down Lot's door.

These angels tell Lot to take his family from the city. When he hesitates, the angels grab his arm and force his departure. They tell Lot's family not to look back, but Lot's wife disobeys. Consequently, God turns her into a pillar of salt. Sodom and her sister city, Gomorrah, are burned to ruins.

While exiled in local mountains, Lot's daughters fear their isolation will stop them from marrying and having children. To rectify this situation, they conspire to have relations with their drunken and unknowing father. The first daughter gets pregnant, and she gives birth to a son who would beget the Moabites. The second daughter gives birth to a son who fathers the Ammonites (Gen 19).

Then, the Genesis story returns to Abraham and Sarah. The king of Gerar (a city between Canaan and Egypt) sought to bed Sarah. Abraham once more says she is his sister. When the king

Genesis

becomes aware of Abraham's ruse, he sends her back to her husband and gives him land on which to live (Gen 20). Later Abraham and Sarah have Isaac.

Sarah wants Abraham's lineage to descend through Isaac, not Ishmael, so she sends the maid Hagar and Ishmael, her son, away. The Lord promises them protection and a nation. King Abimelech, leader of the Philistine city of Gerar, makes a covenant to deal fairly with Abraham. Abraham agrees (Gen 21).

God tests Abraham's steadfastness. He asks Abraham to sacrifice his son Isaac. Just as he is about to strike Isaac, God stops him and promises him many children. Then, Sarah dies at 127 years old.

After Abraham and Sarah's saga ends with Sarah's death, the Genesis account moves to the next generation with Abraham seeking a wife for Isaac by sending a servant to Nahor in Mesopotamia. A servant is sent to wait at a community well to select the first woman to set down a jar. This woman is Rebekah, who eventually agrees to wed Isaac (Gen 22–24).[4] Also, Abraham takes another wife, Keturah, who provides him with many children. Figure 3.3 identifies Abraham's wives and Isaac and Ishmael's mothers.

Figure 3.3: Isaac and Ismael's father and mothers

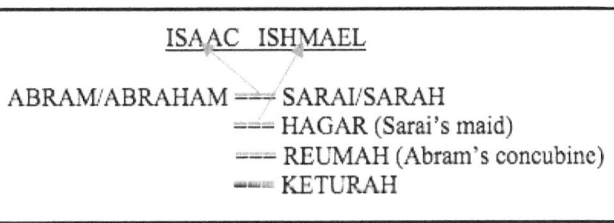

When Abraham dies, Isaac and Ishmael bury him in Machpelah's Cave with his wife Sarah. Although Ishmael is older than Isaac, Isaac receives all of Abraham's possessions.

Finally, Isaac and Rebekah have twins Esau and Jacob. Isaac loves Esau; Rebekah loves Jacob. At one point, Esau returns home hungry and dying, and he asks Jacob for food. In what many

---

4. Rebekah was Bethel's daughter and Laban's sister.

consider a dastardly act, Jacob asks Esau to yield his birthright to him. Esau does. Consequently, Jacob receives Isaac's possessions and lineage (Gen 25).

History is repeated when a Hebrew wife catches the attention of an Egyptian pharaoh and her husband denies their relationship.[5] This time it was Rebekah who caught King Abimelech's eye, and Isaac disowns his wife. When the king learns of the hoax, although angered, Abimelech does not punish Isaac, who remains in Gerar and prospers while the Philistines grow envious of his success. King Abimelech understands that God is on Isaac's side, and so makes a covenant of peace with him. Lastly, when Esau is forty years old, he marries Judith, and the couple bring undisclosed grief to Isaac and Rebekah (Gen 26).

The story flips back to brothers Esau and Jacob. When Isaac asked for his last meal from Esau, Rebekah directed Jacob to pretend to be Esau. He complied and placed a fleece over himself to mimic Esau's hairiness. It worked. Isaac blessed Jacob thinking he was Esau. When Esau learns about the deception, he threatens to kill Jacob. Rebekah tells Jacob to leave Beersheba for Haran until Esau cools off. Along the way, Jacob dreams of a ladder descending from heaven, and God promises him a parcel of land (Gen 27–28). (Genesis 36 says Esau left the land he shared with Jacob in Canaan because it could not sustain their flocks.)

Then Genesis goes into greater detail with Jacob's life. A man introduces him to Rachel, who bedazzles him. Although Jacob asks Laban, Rachel's father, for her hand, Laban gives him, instead, older daughter Leah (the marital norm at that time). Laban strikes a deal with Jacob: If Jacob works for him for seven years, he could marry Rachel. Jacob agrees. In the seventh year, Jacob goes to claim Rachel. Laban, however, deceives Jacob and brings Leah to his bed.

Later, Jacob marries and has children with both women but, at first, God does not "open" Rachel's womb (Gen 29). She grows jealous, and ultimately God opens her womb. She gives birth to Joseph.

---

5. Abraham pulled the same stunt with the king in Gerar (Gen 20). Father and later, son, denied their marital relationships in the face of power.

Genesis

Jacob and his family continue to live in his father-in-law's territory. Laban and Jacob prosper, but Jacob yearns for his homeland of Canaan and leaves without Laban's blessing. The two men had been having issues, but Laban seeks to settle them with a covenant. They agree, but while traveling to Canaan, Jacob meets a stranger (God) who wrestles with him to a draw. When God asks Jacob his name, he changes it to Israel (Gen 32–33).

The story continues with Israel's (previously known as Jacob) family. Leah and Israel have a daughter Dinah. She meets Shechem, and they initially fall in love, but he rapes her.[6] Hamor, Shechem's father, informs Israel of his son's dastardly act but asks if their other sons and daughters could marry to maintain intergroup relations. If Hamor agreed to circumcise his male offspring, Israel would approve the pact. Hamor complies. Finally, Jacob's sons Simeon and Levi could not let their sister's molestation go unpunished, so they murder every male and take their wealth (Gen 30–33).

Before her death, Rachel bears Ben-oni, who Israel renames Benjamin. After Rachel's burial, Israel proceedes to the Tower of Eder, where his son, Reuben, lies with Bilhah, Israel's concubine. (Gen 34–35).

The Genesis story continues by pointing out Israel's extraordinary affection for his son, Joseph, marking this closeness by making his son a colorful tunic. The story moves to Joseph's relationship with his brothers.

The young man has dreams that he would rule over his brothers. They become jealous and plot to kill Joseph. Reuben opposes this scheme, so, instead, he and his brothers sell Joseph into Egyptian slavery (Gen 37).

Family relationships emerge again in Genesis 38 when the story shifts to Judah, another of Israel's sons. He marries Shua, who bears three sons, Er, Onan, and Shelah. God kills Er for his wickedness. Judah tells Onan to wed his deceased brother's wife, Tamar,

---

6. Hamor, Shechem's father, was a Hivite who sold the land to Jacob for his burial ground. Hamor wanted his people and Jacob's to engage in social and commercial exchanges.

Part III: First Five Books of the Bible

but Onan refuses because custom would deny their children his name.

Consequently, Onan spills his seed on the ground. God sees him do this and kills him. Judah tells Tamar to wait for Shelah to come of age to marry him. Meanwhile, Judah's wife dies and his daughter-in-law seduces him. This produces twins, Perez and Zerah (Gen 38).

The Genesis author moves the story back to Egypt and Joseph. The pharaoh's wife tries to seduce Joseph, but he turns her down. She lies and claims Joseph approached her. Accordingly, the sovereign commits Joseph to prison, where he meets a cupbearer and a baker. Each has a dream that Joseph interprets and then comes true: the cupbearer is freed and the baker hung. Later, the pharaoh has a dream. The cupbearer tells him about Joseph's talent and Joseph is brought to interpret the pharaoh's dream. Joseph says Egypt would experience seven years of plenty, followed by seven years of famine. These events take place and Joseph is rewarded by the Egyptian ruler.(Gen 39–41).

When famine hits not only Egypt but also Canaan, Israel sends his sons to Egypt to secure grain for his people. Joseph's brothers did not know he was alive or that he had acquired high status in the Egyptian hierarchy. When they arrive in Egypt, they do not recognize Joseph but Joseph knows them. He dispatches his brothers to Canaan but holds Simeon and demands they bring back Benjamin to him. Joseph wants Benjamin to demonstrate that the brothers are sincere about buying grain.

Before leaving Egypt, the Canaanites leave money with Joseph, an appropriate gesture. He, however, takes this money and hides it among his brother's possessions. When they realize they still had the money, the brothers hurry to return it to Joseph in fear he would think they stole it. When they meet, Joseph reveals his identity. He cries, his brothers rejoice, and they celebrate.

Before Genesis ends, Joseph takes his first son, Manasseh, and his second son, Ephraim, to visit his father. Israel blesses Ephraim over Manasseh, which violates the custom of sanctifying the first son. Israel instructs Joseph to bury him in the cave at Machpelah in Canaan with his ancestors after his death. Joseph dies at 110 years old and is buried in Egypt. Genesis ends here (Gen 42–50).

Who?

Genesis reads like a Russian novel with a cast of thousands. It has more than 300 individuals and several groups (e.g., Hittites). (See Figures 3.4 and 3.5.)[7]

Figure 3.4. Genesis genealogy from Adam to Noah and his sons (Gen 1–9)

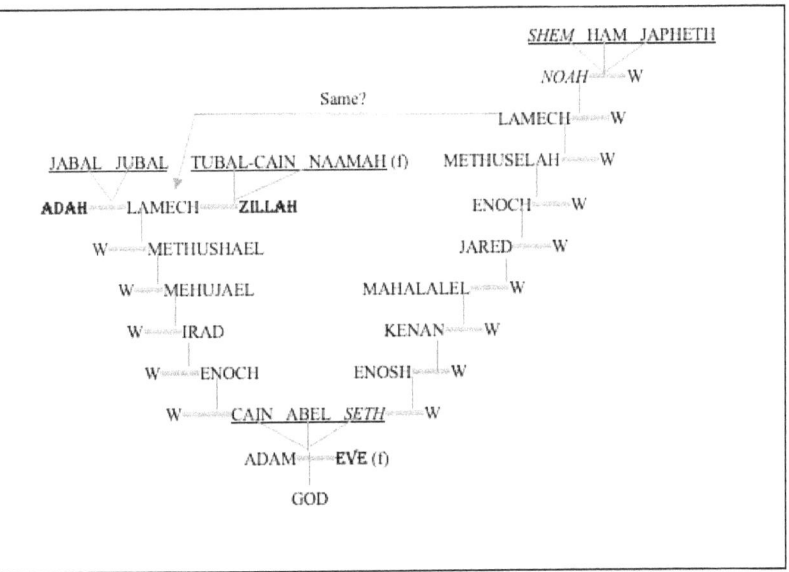

---

7. For Fig. 3.4: Names in italics have a line of descent to Jesus. Names in Algerian font are women. "W" indicates an unnamed wife. Underlined names are siblings.

For Fig. 3.5: Names in italics follow a line of biblical descent. Names in Algerian font are women. Symbols mean: arrows or dashes indicate "married to," a box means siblings a line stands for "related to." Black capitalized names are the twelve tribes of Israel.

Part III: First Five Books of the Bible

Figure 3.5. Genealogy from Shem through Abraham to Joseph and Ephraim
(Gen 10–50)

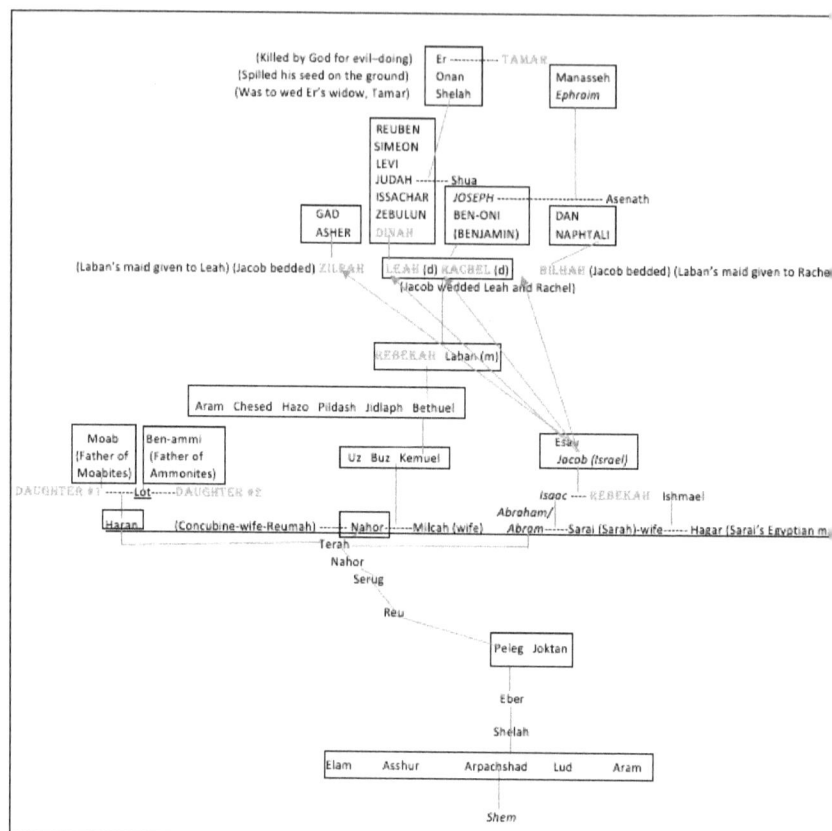

Captivating as these numbers may be, it is more important to know how these people were related. At the very beginning of the Genesis story, a curious question arises in a contemporary mind: How did humans advance their species without engaging in incest? As stated in Genesis, Adam and Eve conceived three sons: Cain, Abel, and Seth.[8] So, then, how did these sons have children without having intercourse with their mother?

---

8. When specific people are named who gave birth, mention is often made that "they had other sons and daughters."

Genesis

More than one thousand years later, when Abraham and his brothers, Haran and Nahor, walk on Earth, more questions surface. For instance, Haran's son Lot had two daughters. When Lot's daughters took refuge in the hill country with their father after God sacked Sodom and Gomorrah, they feared they would remain childless because there weren't any marital partners. So, they plotted together to get pregnant by their father—explicit incest.

Nahor and Abraham were married and both had concubines; that is, they had *polygamous* relationships. As for Abraham, his polygamous bond produced Ishmael, while relations with his wife bore Isaac. In later life, when Abraham was dying, he passed his lineage to Isaac, not Ishmael, since he was a product of a higher relationship. When Isaac reached the marriage age, he wed his cousin Rebekah. Biblical figures often kept their sexual and marriage relationships with their families.

When Isaac's son Jacob attained the age of marriage, he fell for Rachel. She, however, was younger than her sister, Leah. The girls' father, Laban, consequently would not permit Jacob to marry Rachel, per marital custom. Instead, he presented Jacob with a deal. Work for Laban for seven years, then he could marry Rachel (How many today would take this deal?). This marital story gets still more complicated. Jacob ended up marring Leah even after fulfilling the deal, and she gave her maid, Zilpah, to him. Later, Jacob married his love, Rachel, and she, too, gave her maid, Bilhah, to him. These polygamous relationships produced twelve males who formed the twelve tribes of Israel.

One of Rachel and Jacob's sons was Judah; he had three sons: Er, Onan, and Shelah. Er was evil, so God killed him. Judah betrothed Er's widow, Tamar, to Onan, but he did not want to marry his deceased brother's wife. Why? People would know these children under his dead brother's name. So Onan "spilled his seed on the ground" rather than impregnating Tamar. Thus, Onan protected his personal lineage.

Several people state that God's anger toward Onan was because he masturbated. Others, however, hold that Onan's sin was sociological. He refused to marry his sister-in-law, as directed by his father. In this view, family relations were an essential factor.

Finally, Joseph was one of Rachel and Jacob/Israel's sons, married, and had, at least, two sons (Manasseh and Ephraim). When Joseph was dying, he chose his second son (Ephraim) over his first son (Manasseh) to pass on his lineage. This action defied the customs of the time.

Drawing back our sociological lens on Genesis, we note that less than ten percent of the people in this book are females. The average age among individuals is 541 years old, while the median age is 451 years old. Joseph is the youngest at 110 years old, and Methuselah is the most senior at 969 years old.

Specific and general occupational statuses included:

- About ten kings,
- At least one pharaoh,
- Sixteen chiefs,
- A priest,
- A prince/sheik (i.e., Shechem, Gen 33),
- A king's advisor (i.e., Ahuzzath, Gen 26),
- An army commander (i.e., Philcol, Gen 26), and
- Captain Potiphar of Egypt's royal guard (Gen 37).

There were shepherds, farmers, maids, concubines, a cupboard servant, and a baker. Having so many occupational statuses demonstrates that biblical societies were more complex than simple.

Jacob/Israel's offspring from his two wives (Leah and Rachel) and his two concubines (Zilpah and Bilhah) produced the twelve tribes of Israel.

- Zilpah produced Gad and Asher.
- Leah bore Reuben, Simeon, Levi, Judah, Issachar, and Zebulun.[9]

---

9. She gave birth to a daughter, Dinah.

- Rachel had Joseph and Ben-oni (Benjamin).
- Bilhah gave birth to Dan and Naphtali.

From Adam to Noah and on to Abraham, Isaac, and Jacob (Israel), the twelve tribes of Israel, the Hebrew people, took possession of the Promised Land of Canaan. Since these tribes were named after Israel (God changed Jacob's name), the Hebrew people became known as Israelites.

What?

Subject matter in Genesis has three parts:

- Creation,
- Destruction, and
- Reconstruction and Covenants.

Creation

The very word "Genesis" means beginning. This first book of the Bible chronicles the development of the physical world and its social domain. In six days, God created light out of darkness, and the heavens along with Earth and its contents—land, sea, vegetation, and animals. Next, he created man; and out of man, woman. Adam and Eve are progenitors of the human race. They created Cain, Abel, and later Seth. From these first humans came the social world we now inhabit.

Destruction

Adam and Eve lived happily in Paradise until they disobeyed God's command not to eat from the tree of knowledge of good and evil. When they did, humans became self-conscious. They no longer experienced themselves *of* the world. They were now *in* the world. They felt disconnected from each other, other creatures, and God himself. This alienation from God brought destruction to Earth. Until eating the fruit, Adam and Eve had conformed to God's norms, but destruction (i.e., negative sanction) ensued when they deviated from them.

According to Genesis, God created a good world, but when Adam and Eve disobeyed him, God banished them from the Garden of Eden. They became mortal, understanding there was good and evil and developing the awareness that they could choose between them.

Over time, God witnessed humans making bad choices and got angry with them. He wanted to destroy the world, so he brought rain that lasted forty days and forty nights. This deluge created a flood that covered Earth.

Reconstruction and Covenants

God, however, recognized Noah was a righteous man. He spared him, his family, and Earth's creatures from the Great Flood. The Lord dried out the land, and human, animal, and vegetative life returned. Then humankind procreated, wandering what is now the Middle East, searching for peace, prosperity, and land. Humans developed from large families into tribes and later into nations, such as Assyria and Israel. To keep track of this early development, Genesis recorded the descendants of Adam, Noah, Shem (Noah's son), and generations later, Abraham, Isaac (Abraham's son), Jacob (Isaac's son), and Joseph (Jacob's son). Figure 3.6 traces biblical descent from the first human—Adam—to the last person mentioned in Genesis—Joseph.

Figure 3.6. Tracing generations from Adam to Joseph

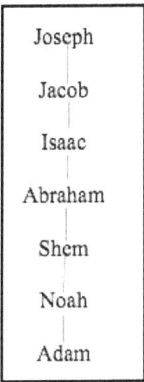

Genesis records the developing relationship between God and his chosen people (Israelites). As these people honored him, the Lord guided and protected them. When they disobeyed him, however, he brought havoc upon them. To avoid catastrophe, God and his people entered into a covenant, or binding agreement, to mark their matured relationship. The book of Genesis records four covenants. These were agreements between, primarily, God and people, but also among people. In Genesis 9, God promised Noah he would not inflict another worldwide flood on Earth. Essentially, he was withdrawing divine intervention from the earthly physical realm. In another covenant (Gen 17), God promised Abraham many children, even into old age, and a nation.

The next two covenants were among people. In the first, King Abimelech recognized the the Lord had blessed Isaac and, consequently, the king sought peace with him (Gen 26). Then, Laban, Jacob's father-in-law, made peace with Jacob at Mizpah, where they stacked rocks to commemorate the deal (Gen 31).

God gave the chosen people (Israelites) a Diagram of Social Situations by which these people were to live with the diety with whom they had made a covenant. The deity gave the chosen people (Israelites) a Diagram of Social Situations by which these people were to live with God. Then these people modeled this diagram for

Part III: First Five Books of the Bible

life among themselves. For example, God said not to take his name in vain. Israelites advanced ordinances that bound their citizens to behave in respectful ways.

When?

Genesis covers the time from the inception of the world to Joseph's death in 1695 BCE. Twenty-five generations passed between Adam's creation and Joseph's passing. The timelines in Figures 3.7 and 3.8 cite notable characters and events.

Figure 3.7: Notable people in Genesis

PERSON	YEAR (BCE) BORN	DIED	AGE
ADAM	4004	3074	930 years old
SETH	3874	2962	912
METHUSELAH	3317	2348	969
NOAH	2948	1998	950
SHEM (Noah's son)	2446	1846	600
TERAH (Abraham's father)	2126	1921	205
ABRAM/ ABRAHAM	2056	1881	175
ISAAC (Abraham's son)	1956	1776	180
JACOB/ISRAEL (Isaac's son)	1896	1749	147
JOSEPH (Jacob's son)	1805	1695	110

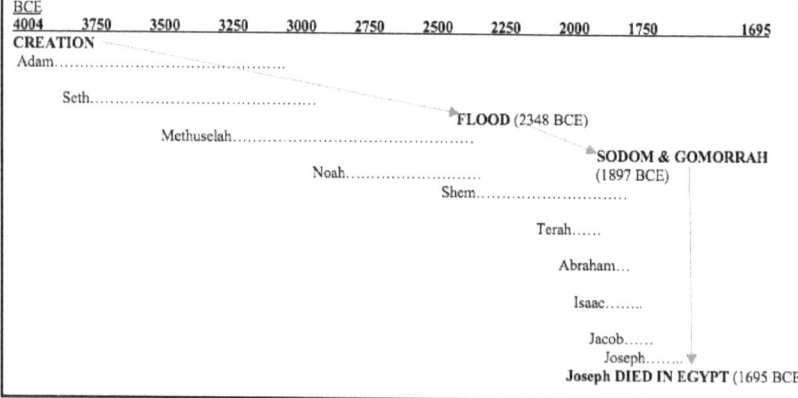

Figure 3.8: Timeline of people and events in Figure 3.7

Genesis

Figures 3.7 and 3.8 show that 1,656 years passed between Adam's creation and Noah's death. From the Great Flood to Sodom and Gomorrah's destruction, 451 years passed. After God decimated these cities to Joseph's death, 202 years passed. Thus, fifty chapters in the book of Genesis cover roughly 2,300 years.

Where?

It all began in the Garden of Eden. But where was this place? By most accounts, Adam and Eve resided on a "fertile crescent" between the Tigris and Euphrates rivers in Mesopotamia (meaning "place between two rivers"). These rivers run parallel to each other from their sources in eastern Turkey and flow southeast through present-day Syria and Iraq into the Persian Gulf.

Map 3.1: Tigris and Euphrates Rivers with Garden of Eden

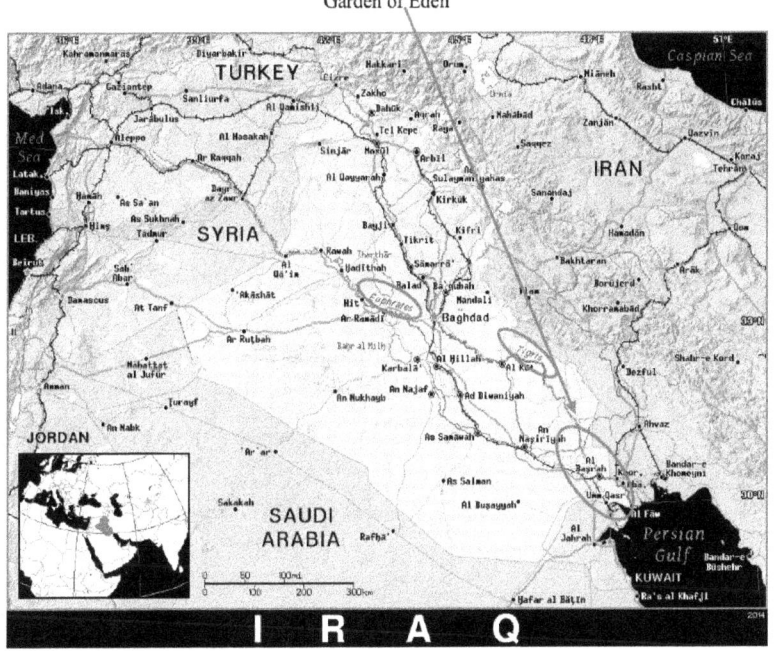

Source: Ian Macky, PAT

Part III: First Five Books of the Bible

After Adam and Eve's fall from God's grace and expulsion from the Garden of Eden, the Genesis story continues in Mesopotamia until the Great Flood destroyed Earth. After the waters receded, Noah's Ark landed on Mt. Ararat in Turkey, north of Mesopotamia. This site is approximately 1,000 miles north of the potential site of Eden. It took about 1,600 years of migration to cover this territory.

Map 3.2 Mt. Ararat in Turkey

Source: Ian Macky, PAT

Then Noah's descendants settled in the land of Shinar (Babylonia). This place was where Nimrod established his kingdom, which included the Tower of Babel.

50

Map 3.3: Land of Shinar and Tower of Babel

Source: Ian Macky, PAT

Later, Terah fathered Abram (Abraham), Nahor, and Haran. Haran fathered Lot. When Abraham was seventy-five years old, Terah took Lot and Terah's daughter-in-law (Sarai/Sarah, Abraham's wife) from the Chaldeans and went to Canaan, but they only made it to Haran and settled there. Terah died when he was 205 years old.

Part III: First Five Books of the Bible

Map 3.4: Canaan, Abraham's journey, and the Chaldeans

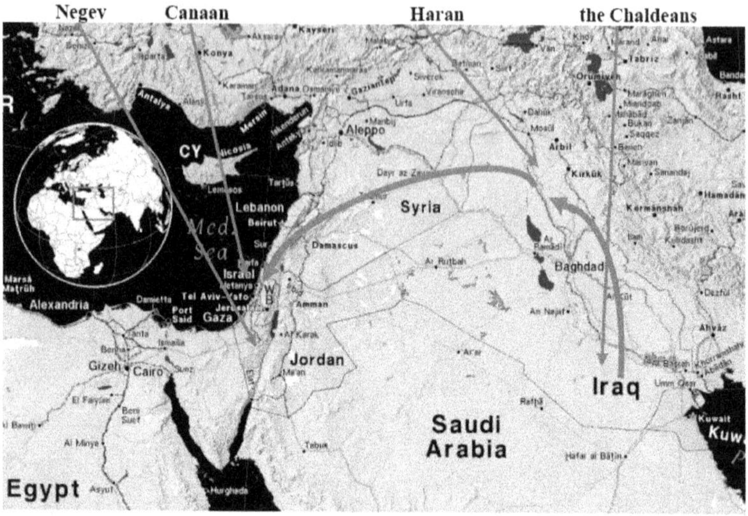

Source: Ian Macky, PAT

Afterward, God told Abraham to proceed to Canaan (the Promised Land). As he approached the Promised Land with his wife and nephew (Lot), Canaanites living there came into view (see Map 3.4). Abram headed toward the Negev (an arid land in southern Canaan, today's Israel) but stopped after learning there was a great famine. He redirected his people toward Egypt. When they arrived, the pharaoh made a play for Sarai. God found out, and he brought plagues on the Egyptians. When the pharaoh learned the truth about Sarai, he expelled Abraham and his people from Egypt. Abraham, Sarai, and Lot left Egypt and again went to the Negev.

Up to this point in the biblical narrative, Sarai had not conceived a child. Later, the Lord made two promises to Abraham: His wife would give birth to a son, and he would give him land (Canaan) for the Hebrews that would grow into a great nation.

The story shifts to men in Sodom who sought other men staying at Lot's home. God told Lot to flee the city before he destroyed it. After they escaped from the city's destruction, Lot and

Genesis

his family lived in the nearby mountains. His daughters feared they would never have children, so they seduced their father to get pregnant. One daughter gave birth to Moab, father of the Moabites. The other daughter sired Ben-ammi, father of the Ammonites.

Map 3.5: Gomorrah, Sodom, Moabites, and Ammonites

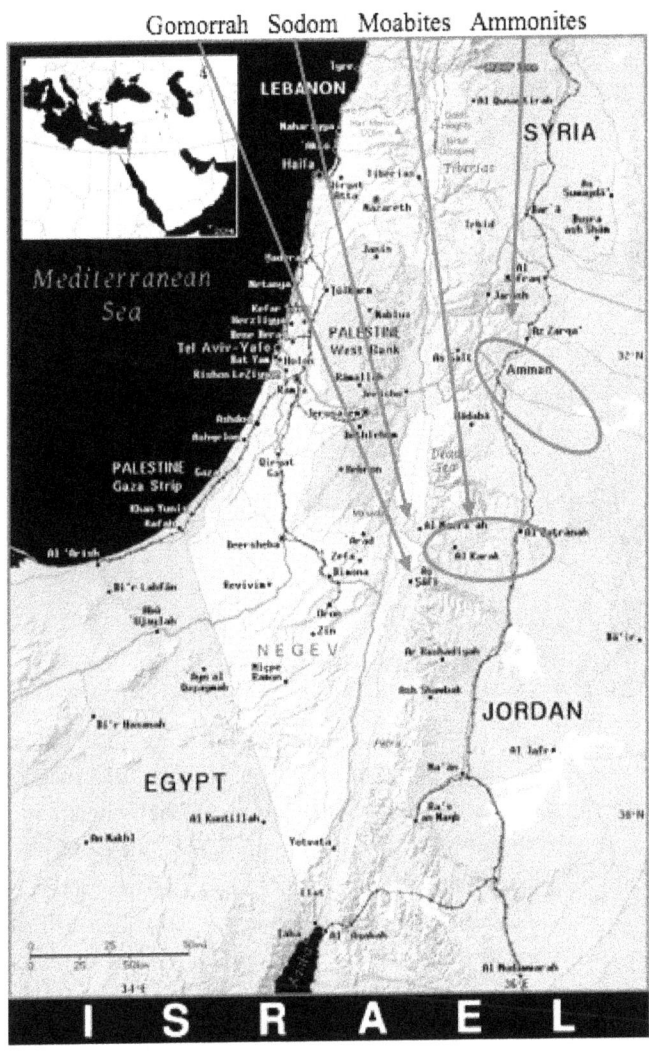

Source: Ian Macky, PAT

Part III: First Five Books of the Bible

Next the Genesis story follows Isaac's twin sons, Esau and Jacob. Jacob left Beersheba for Haran to seek a wife from Laban's daughters. After years of servitude with Laban, he left Laban's territory with a coterie of women. They crossed the Euphrates River and headed toward the Promised Land. On his journey to God's Promised Land, Jacob wrestled to a draw with a man (God). This man changed Jacob's name to Israel. Genesis set the scene for entry into Canaan, but there was one detour.

Map 3.6: Jacob's route from Beersheba to Haran and his return from Paddan-aram to Canaan (Israel)

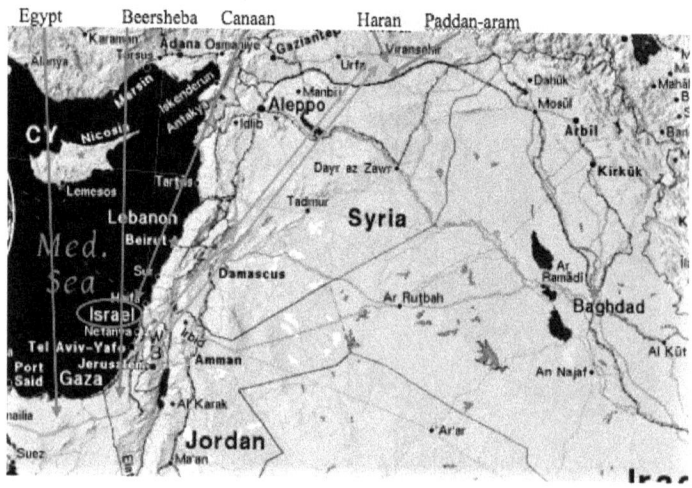

Source: Ian Macky, PAT

Joseph was Israel's (Jacob's) favorite son, so Joseph's brothers were jealous and plotted to kill him. Reuben, one of Joseph's brothers, opposed the plot. Consequently, Joseph's brothers sold him to a tribe that took him to Egypt. Once there, Joseph rose within the pharaoh's hierarchy because he successfully interpreted the pharaoh's dream that predicted famine. Israel fled to Canaan because of famine there, too, and entered Egypt. After reconciling with his family, Joseph convinced the pharaoh to accept Israel and his entire family. Genesis ends with the chosen people (Israelites) in Egypt, where they resided for about 400 years.

Genesis

Map 3.7: Canaan (Israel) and Egypt

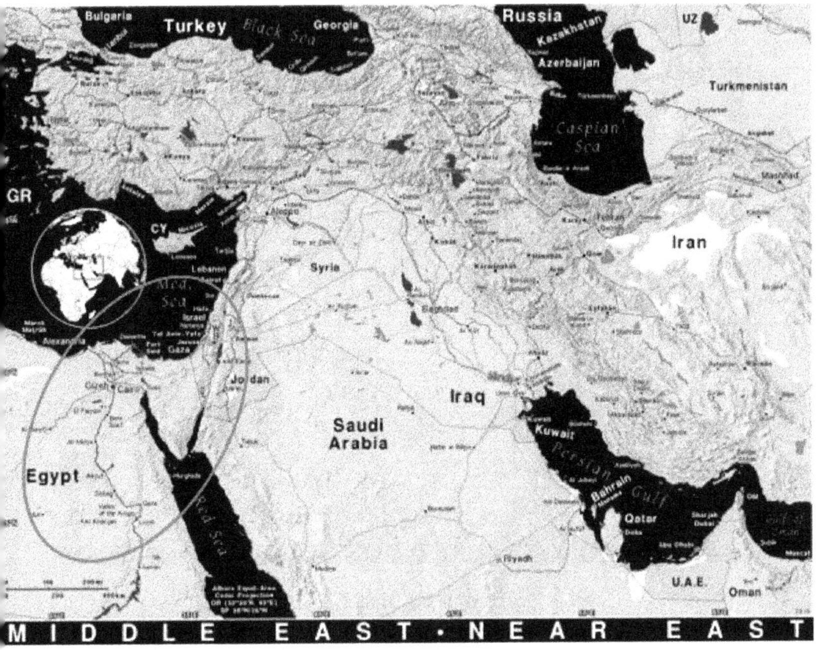

Source: Ian Macky, PAT

Map 3.8 shows where the entire Genesis story took place on a modern map.

Part III: First Five Books of the Bible

Map 3.8: Location of the Genesis story on a modern-day map

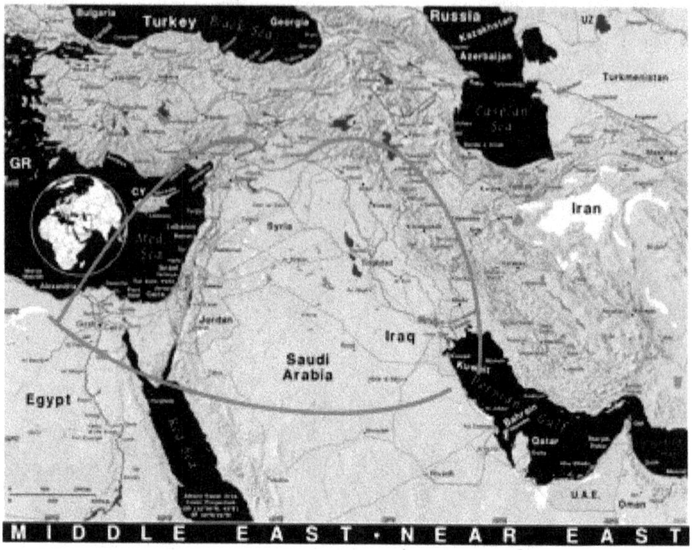

Source: Ian Macky, PAT

According to Genesis, Adam and Eve lived in the Garden of Eden in Mesopotamia. In the last book of the New Testament, Revelations, Jesus talked about arriving in New Jerusalem (heaven). Thus, the Bible (Old and New testaments) spanned the territory from this world into the next. Biblical space, consequently, stretches from the Middle East into somewhere in eternity.

Why?

Genesis is a sacred narrative that describes the physical creation of the world. It also identifies individuals (e.g., Adam, Noah, and Abraham) blessed and chosen by God to populate the planet and praise the Lord.

Specifically, Genesis answered:

1. Who created the world? God

2. How were men and women created? God made them

3. How did sin enter the world? Adam and Eve disobeyed God

4. What retribution do sinners receive? Banishment from Paradise and assumption of mortal life

5. Who were Adam's descendants? Significantly, Noah, Abraham, Isaac, Jacob, and Joseph, and

6. What was their nation? Israel.

Essentially, Genesis is a book about creation, destruction, and rebirth. So, "In the beginning . . ." which are the first three words of the Bible, open an epic that describes the tribulations, treachery, and triumph of human life.

How?

The author of Genesis, believed to be Moses, was a problematic writer. Scholars assume Moses wrote the first five books of the Bible, which are known as the Torah or Pentateuch. Many claim Moses wrote Genesis sometime between 1445 and 1405 BCE.[10]

Genesis can be challenging to read. First, its fifty chapters cover over 300 people. Keeping track of all of them can be difficult. In Genesis 10, for example, Noah's descendants are listed in thirty-two verses. These verses cite approximately sixty-four names for readers to digest.

Moreover, names repeat themselves in different sections of the book. For instance, Genesis 4:18, 5:21, and 5:25 cite Methuselah and Lamech. Second, sentence structure is archaic, making it difficult for modern readers to understand. For example, in Genesis 11:

> Shem was one hundred years old and became the father of Arpachshad two years after the flood, and Shem lived five hundred years after he became the father of Arpachshad, and he had *other* sons and daughters.

10. Hodge and Mortenson. "Did Moses Write Genesis?"

Part III: First Five Books of the Bible

A modern author might have written it this way:

> Two years after the flood, Shem, who was 100 years old, fathered Arpachshad. He lived another 500 years and had other sons and daughters.

Contemporary readers unfamiliar with people and places presented in the narrative raise a third concern. Sometimes a person and site are given the same name, such as Haran, which is a person and city. Having the same name for a person and a location can confuse and, accordingly, frustrate a bibliophile and inhibit reading further.

The structure of the Genesis story raises a more fundamental problem. Often, episodes occur without reference to when they happen. Did it happen right away, months, or years later? For instance, in chapter two, God creates man and woman. Then chapter three records the fall of man. But there is no mention of how long after Creation the fall happened—was it days, years, or centuries?

Additionally, too many names cited together made it challenging to comprehend them. In two adjourning and short chapters, Gen 10–11, Noah's and Shem's (one of Noah's sons) descendants totaled eighty people. Only after re-reading verses constructed with names of people and places could one sort out its complexity. For example, Gen 10:8–14 read:

> Now Cush became the father of Nimrod; he became a mighty one on earth. He was a mighty hunter before the Lord; therefore, it is said, "Like Nimrod, a mighty hunter before the Lord." The beginning of his kingdom was Babel and Erech and Accad and Calneh, in the land of Shinar. From that land, he went forth into Assyria, and built Nineveh and Rehoboth-Ir and Calah, and Resen between Nineveh and Calah; that is the great city. Mizraim became the father of Ludim and Anamim and Lehabim and Naphtuhim and Pathrusim and Casluhim (from which came the Philistines) and Caphtorim.

In seven verses, there are nine individuals' names, eight cities, land, country, and groups cited. A novice Bible reader cannot comprehend so much and so varied information. Moreover, twelve times "and" is used where comas would have eased understanding.

Chapter 4

Exodus

Who? What? When? Where? Why? How?

Summary of the Book of Exodus

GENESIS OPENS WITH THE creation of the world and ends with Israel/Jacob and Joseph's deaths. Exodus means "to exit" or "to leave." The Israelites left Egypt and their slavery. Forty chapters with 1,213 verses tell this story. The book, however, features more than a departure. It reads like a woodworker's and furniture designer's manuals. For example, God directs Moses to construct a table:

> ... acacia wood, two cubits long and a cubit wide and one and a half cubits high. You shall overlay it with pure gold and make a gold border around it. You shall make four gold rings for it and put rings on the four corners which are on its four feet. (Exod 25:23–24; 26)

Forty-five percent of verses in Exodus concern the construction of a sanctuary and its interior furnishings. Another approximately twelve percent outline God's rules for the Israelites, while the remaining verses depict the Israelites' time in and leaving Egypt.

Exodus

When Genesis ended, Joseph was an Egyptian ruler. At the beginning of Exodus, the Israelites are Egyptian slaves. How did they move from favored status to servitude?

A new pharaoh, unaware of Joseph's status, rules Egypt. Israelites' numbers have increased dramatically during this pharaoh's reign. Consequently, they threaten Egyptian land, property, and wealth. Egyptians want to suppress the Israelites. Moreover, the pharaoh tells Hebrew midwives to kill newly born Israelite males to control a rise in their population. Egyptians use slavery and infanticide as mechanisms of social control.

A Levite (i.e., a descendant of one of Israel's/Jacob's twelve sons) couple have a child.[1] They hide him from Egyptian slaughter when his mother puts him into a basket by the Nile River. Pharaoh's daughter and her maids find him. They name him Moses.

Figure 4.1: Moses' ancestors

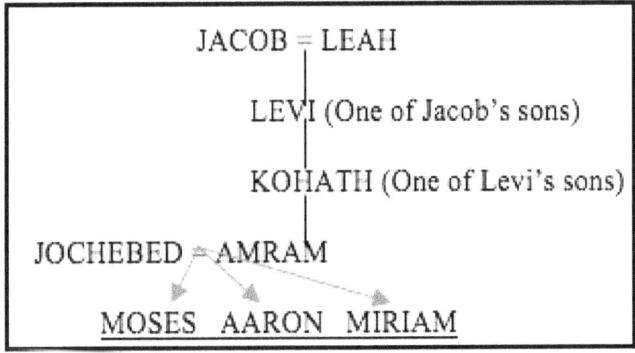

Later, Moses witnesses an Egyptian beating an Israelite. Moses kills the Egyptian and buries him. The next day he observes two Israelites fighting, and he chastises them. These angry Israelites tell Moses they saw him kill an Egyptian. Fearing retribution from the pharaoh, Moses leaves Egypt for Midian. While there, he aids the daughters of Jethro, a Midian priest, who were being mistreated by

---

1. As discussed above, God changed Jacob's name to Israel. Thus, descendants of Jacob's twelve sons formed the twelve tribes of the nation of Israel.

shepherds. In gratitude, Jethro offers Moses one of his daughters. Moses and Zipporah marry and have a son, Gershom. Sometime later, the pharaoh dies, and the Israelites call out to God to free them. Remembering his covenant with the Israelites, God "took notice of them" (Exod 1–2).

Later, as an adult, Moses is attending his flock near Horeb (Mt. Sinai) when he notices a burning bush that was not consumed by its flames. The Lord speaks from the bush and directs Moses not to look directly at him. He claims to be the God of Abraham, Isaac, and Jacob. God tells Moses that he is aware of his people suffering in Egypt, promises to bring them to a land of milk and honey, and directs Moses to lead them there.

Overwhelmed by God's directive, Moses begs God to release him from this duty. God persists while offering assistance to Moses. Moses asks God what to say when the Israelites ask him by what authority they were to follow him. God says to tell them, "I AM WHO I AM. I am the Lord of Abraham, Isaac, and Jacob" (Exod 3:14). God tells Moses to go with the elders to the pharaoh and ask him to let His people go. Then God directs Moses to tell every woman to ask their neighbor for any silver, gold articles, and clothing they had plundered from Egyptians.

Moses asks God what to do if the pharaoh refused to release the Israelites. God tells him to: throw a staff on the ground, which would turn into a serpent; put his hand into his chest, and it would turn leprous; and take Nile River water, pour it on the ground, and it would become blood (Exod 4:2–9).

Moses remains unsure, but God reassures him by offering the assistance of his articulate brother, Aaron. Lastly, God hardens the pharaoh's heart to Moses' request for freedom (Exod 3–4). (The narrative then diverges to listing the heads of Israel.)

Exodus 7 opens with the theme of Moses' indecision and God's reassurance of him. Aaron is eighty-three years old and Moses is eighty when they approach the pharaoh. Moses throws his staff on the ground. It turns into a serpent. Then he turns water into blood. The pharaoh is undeterred because his magicians can perform the same feats. Moses releases frogs over the land, gnats,

Exodus

and then flies. The pharaoh's magicians replicate Moses' acts. Moses continues his demand to let the Israelites go. The pharaoh's heart is hardened. Afterward, cattle die; boils form on men and beasts; hail falls from the sky and kills vegetation; locusts come; darkness falls over the land; and God slays firstborn humans and animals as the last plague. Still, the pharaoh fails to release the Israelites from bondage (Exod 7–11).

After the author of Exodus presents why the Israelites want to flee Egypt and the plagues by which they sought to convince the pharaoh to let them go, the narrator shifts to describing a significant Hebrew religious day.

God establishes Abib as the first month of the year, during which each Israelite household should slaughter a lamb or goat and follow these directions:

1. An animal must be an unblemished, one-year-old male. They ate the meat with unleavened bread and bitter herbs and used some of its blood to mark their houses' doorposts and lintel (beam).
2. They must eat unleavened bread for seven days. They must remove leavened bread from houses on the first day. This Feast of Unleavened Bread symbolizes the day God brought them out of Egypt.
3. No foreigners can partake of the feast, but every circumcised, purchased slave could participate in the banquet. They could not eat flesh outside their house nor break any bones.

This ritual was *Passover*—commemorating the night when God passes over Israelite-marked houses and killed every Egyptian firstborn male and animal (Exod 12). The Israelites obey God, and he strikes down Egyptians. After living in Egypt for 430 years, the Israelites loot the Egyptians, and about 600,000 of them leave Rameses for Succoth in Egypt.

In Exodus 13, the Israelites journey from Egypt, and God tells them to skirt Philistine land (i.e., land adjacent to the Mediterranean Sea) because he fears they would be frightened by the wars going on there and return to Egypt. Consequently, the Israelites proceed through the wilderness along the Red Sea while God guides them with two pillars: a cloud by day and fire by night.

When they reach the Red Sea, Moses lifts his staff and part these waters under God's direction, allowing his people to pass between the parted water. When they reach the other side, Moses hoists his staff, and water falls on the advancing pharaoh's army. Prophetess Miriam (Moses and Aaron's sister) and other women dance with joy as they witnessed the Egyptian army's destruction.

Moses leads the chosen from the Red Sea into the Shur Wilderness. After camping at Elim, they leave for the Sin Wilderness nearby Sinai. These events occurr on the fifteenth day of the second month after they had left Egypt.

The story of the Hebrew exodus from Egypt continues. The Israelites complain about their condition and lament about leaving Egypt. Moses does not know what to do and prays to God for help. The Lord reciprocates by bringing dew, which turns into bread in the morning. Moses tells the Israelites to consume all of it at that time. Some disobey him, trying to hoard the bread, but all the leftovers produce worms.. Also, Moses tells them to take twice as much bread on the sixth day because the following day would be the Sabbath, the day of rest. The people call this substance "manna," which is white and tastes like wafers with honey. They would eat it for forty years before reaching the Promised Land (Exod 14–16).

Next, Joshua (that is, the Israelites' leader after Moses) fields an army against Amalek at Rephidim (The Amalekites were the first enemy the Israelites encountered near the Promised Land). Moses, Aaron, and their companion, Hur, ascend a hill, where Moses raises his hand. When Moses' hands are raised, the Israelites start to win; when his hands are lowered, the tide turns to the Amalekites. Aaron and Hur hold up Moses' hand, and Moses destroys Amalek (Exod 17).

Jethro (Moses' father-in-law) knows God is helping the Israelites. He understands that Moses is overworked judging people's misdeeds, so he suggests he form a group to help. Moses agrees. (Exod 18).

Exodus

The Exodus story changes from an account of the Israelites' plight, leaving Egypt, and wandering in the desert to a description of God's requirements for his adoration and the people's obedience to his will.

Subsequently, God is ready to receive his people on Mt. Sinai and tells Moses to tell them: "He had borne them on eagles' wings and brought them to himself" (Exod 19:4). Only Moses, however, is permitted to ascend the mountain. If anyone else did, they would die. The Israelites are not to engage in sexual relations as an additional act of preparation. Then the Lord bargains with Moses and his people. He would select them as his chosen people and give them a nation if they obeyed his rules, giving them the Ten Commandments (Exod 20):

1. You shall have no other gods.
2. You shall not make an idol for yourself.
3. You shall not worship or serve idols.
4. You shall not take the name of the Lord in vain.
5. Remember the Sabbath, and do not work on this day.
6. Honor your father and mother.
7. You shall not murder.
8. You shall not steal.
9. You shall not bear false witness against your neighbor.
10. You shall not covet your neighbor's possessions nor his wife.

God gives more directions to the Israelites, such as prescriptions for treating slaves (for example, Hebrew slaves would serve seven years and then were to be freed). God promulgates twenty ordinances for personal injuries: a man would die if he killed another; fourteen property rights: a man would pay five oxen for a fox or four sheep for a sheep stolen, destroyed, or sold; and twenty-two sundry laws: a man must pay a dowry if he seduces a virgin who is not engaged to him. Next, God presents three rules for the Sabbath and for land, such as: "sow your land . . . for six years . . .

and in the seventh year let the land rest" (Exod 23:10–11). Then he establishes eight rules for national feasts. For example, during the Feast of Unleavened Bread, the Israelites would eat this bread for seven days during the month of Abib, which celebrates the time they left Egypt.

In sum, God demands the Israelites' allegiance. If they follow only him and his commandments, the Lord would guide them through Amorite, Hittite, and other groups' territories to the Promised Land. God calls Moses, Aaron, Nadab and Abihu (Aaron's first two sons), and seventy Israelite elders to the mountain where he gives Moses the Ten Commandments written on tablets. Moses stays there for forty days and forty nights (Exod 19–24).

God tells Moses that male Israelites must raise tribute, such as gold, silver, and bronze, to furnish a sanctuary where he would dwell and meet his people. He gives Moses sixteen specific directions for constructing and furnishing a tabernacle. For example, God says that Moses should build the Ark of the Covenant with acacia wood 2½ cubits long (one cubit = about 18 inches), 1½ cubit wide, and 1½ cubit high (Exod 25:10). God could meet his people in the ark above a mercy seat located between two cherubim. He could talk to them about his commandments.

The Lord gives directions for constructing an acacia wood table: two cubits long, one cubit wide, and 1½ cubit high (Exod 25:23). God continues his oration with directions for making multiple items, such as a lampstand, curtains, tabernacle boards and sockets, and priests' garments. The Lord directs how to consecrate priests, construct an altar of incense, and prepare incense. He outlines talents he gave to men for building his tent and itemizes an inventory of items for its construction. Together, the Lord gives roughly 160 instructions. Figures 4.2 and 4.3 illustrate the design of the tabernacle and the look of the ark, respectively.

Exodus

Figure 4.2: Court of the Tabernacle

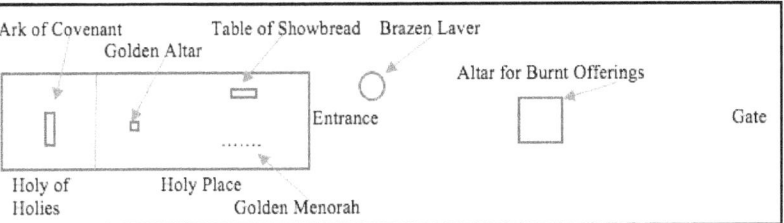

Figure 4.3: Ark of the Covenant

Source: "Ark of the Covenant, Jewish religious symbol." https://www.dreamstime.com/stock-photo-ark-covenant-jewish-religious-symbol-figures-cherubim-isolated-white-background-image92010958.

Lastly, the Sabbath is to be a sign between God and his people. It symbolizes the Lord who has sanctified them. Those who profane this symbol would be either ostracized from the community of believers or die. God establishes the Sabbath to be celebrated forever as a perpetual covenant (Exod 25–31).

Part III: First Five Books of the Bible

Then the story's perspective shifts away from a concern about God's wishes. The focus is now on how badly the Israelites practice their new religion and how God responds.

While Moses is on Mt. Sinai for forty days and nights, the Israelites with him grow impatient and convince Aaron to melt gold into an idol. God sees their evil deed, becomes angry, and compels Moses to chastise them. When Moses sees the golden calf, he throws the two tablets with the Ten Commandments to the ground, and they shatter. Moses asks who was still faithful to the Lord and divides the people accordingly. He directs the faithful to kill every man, woman, and child who did not stand with them. About 3,000 people die that day (Exod 32).

The last part of the Exodus narrative concentrates on God's relationship with Moses and the Israelites (and through them humanity). For example, God tells Moses to go to the Promised Land where an angel would help him drive out Canaanites, Amorites, and others. Map 4.1 cites the location of groups who occupied the Promised Land.

Map 4.1: Land occupied by Canaanites, Amorites, Hittites, Perizzites, Hivites, and Jebusites

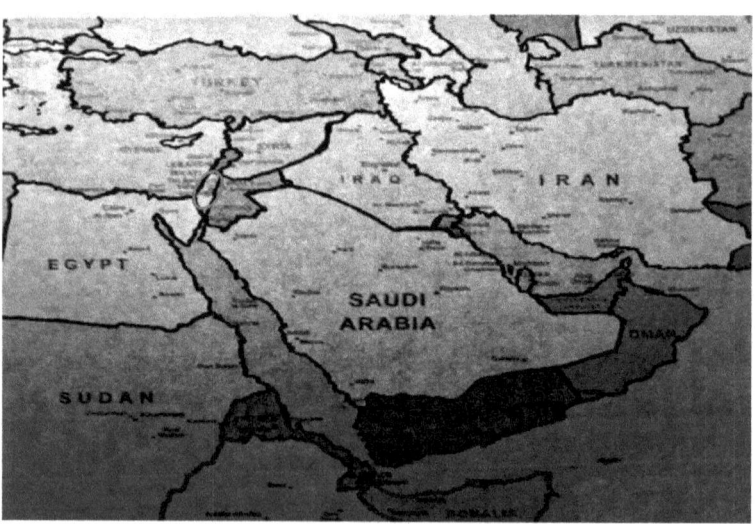

Source: Ian Macky, PAT

Exodus

The last part of the Exodus narrative concentrates on God's relationship with humanity via Moses and the Israelites. Moses goes to see the Lord in his tent. However, God does not permit Moses to see his face though they talk with one another as friends (Exod 33:11). God describes himself as compassionate; gracious; slow to anger; boundless in loving kindness and truth; forgiving of iniquity, transgressions, and sin; and punisher of the guilty, visiting iniquity generation after generation. The Lord says he would make covenants, perform miracles, and drive out Promised Land inhabitants. He warns Israelites not to worship other gods and to avoid making covenants with them.

The Exodus narrative finishes with more construction and garment directions from God. Finally, God gives an accounting of the tabernacle's cost and shows its setup. The story ends.

Who?

Adam was to Noah as Abraham was to Moses. What does this analogy mean?

Adam started the human race, while Noah restarted it after the Great Flood, then Abraham started God's chosen people on their spiritual journey. Moses revived the chosen people when he brought them out of Egyptian slavery and led them to the Promised Land. Thus, Adam and Noah's theme was humanity's physical relationship with Earth, while Abraham and Moses' accounts focused on the chosen people's spiritual relationship with God.

Exodus has ninety-three individuals and sixteen groups in its narrative. Unsurprisingly, the most often-named individual is Moses (276 times), followed by his brother, Aaron (115 times).[2]

Exodus's sex composition parallels Genesis with far more males (seventy) than females (eighteen). The patriarchal character of the Bible continues in its second book.

There is scant mention of ages in Exodus. The book cites only five individuals' ages:

---

2. Clearly the Bible states God's name more times than any human's.

- Levi: lived for 137 years. As the patriarch of Moses' family, he was Moses' great-great-grandfather.
- Kohath: lived for 133 years. He was Moses' great-grandfather.
- Amram: lived until 137 years old. He was Moses' father.
- Aaron: was eighty-three years old when God asked him to help Moses lead Hebrews out of Egypt.
- Moses: was eighty years old when God asked him to lead Hebrews to the Promised Land.

The author lists twenty occupations in Exodus. They span Egyptian society from its lowest to highest levels. At the bottom are hard laborers, field laborers, servants, and slaves, while on its middle strata are freemen, midwives, and wet nurses, and more skilled workers, such as craftsmen, weavers, taskmasters, and supervisors. At the top of Egyptian society are priests, judges, a prince, and pharaohs. The arrangement of these statuses demonstrates an Egyptian *stratified* society, meaning some people had more than others. It was a system of inequality.

Exodus lists families throughout. For instance, Exodus 1:1 names seventy sons of Israel (Jacob) living in Egypt. Afterward, the book announces Moses' birth and his mission, and the Exodus narrator lists the heads of the Israelites.

Finally, the Hebrews lived in Egypt for 430 years—first as free people and later as slaves. Exodus 38:26 records 603,550 men over the age of twenty. They wandered the desert and constructed the tabernacle. Add to this figure women and children, and we can only imagine how many Israelites left Egypt for the Holy Land.

What?

Exodus, reputedly, is the Hebrew story of exiting Egypt, wandering in the wilderness, and arriving at the Promised Land's doorstep. This story, however, represents only a third of the book. The remaining narrative cites rules.

Exodus

Genesis had triple-digit numbers of people in it. Exodus has as many rules. Although Genesis has over 300 people in it, Exodus has about 121 commandments. Thus, Exodus has one-third as many rules as there were people in Genesis.

The Diagram of Social Situations shows how a group or society must physically survive before it can establish a *social structure* with norms and values. So, too, in the Bible, the narrative starts in Genesis with humans "increasing and multiplying." Then, in Exodus, it shows how people received rules from God in order to build a religious society. God's laws fell into two categories. Rules governing people's relationship with:

1. God and
2. Other humans

The first rules shaped the Hebrews' conduct during Passover, which celebrated God's "passing over" Israelites' homes as he slaughtered the firstborn sons of others. Then, the Lord said if the Hebrews obeyed him, acted rightly, and obeyed his commandments, no disease would affect them.

After leaving Egypt and passing through the Red Sea, the Hebrews went through the wilderness and arrived at Mount Sinai. Moses met God on the mountaintop. He gave Moses the Ten Commandments.

Eight out of the Ten Commandments inform the faithful what they should *not* do (i.e., Exod 20:2–7, 10, and 13–17). These commandments identify behaviors situated outside the norms on the Diagram of Social Situations. Keeping the Sabbath holy and honoring fathers and mothers are the only commandments that do not assert a negative.

Then, God handed Moses lists of rules directing humans in their relationships with each other. A focus on personal injuries and property rights dominated the list. In Exodus 21:2–36, 22:1–31, and 23:1–9, the Lord directed how masters were to treat their slaves:

- Free them after seven years of servitude (Exod 21:2).
- Release the wives of slaves (Exod 21:3).

- If a man struck a slave and he or she died, the master would be punished (Exod 21:20), but there was no vengeance (punishment) if the slave survived a day or two because he was the master's property (Exod 21:21).

Rules for an agrarian society are plentiful, too. For example, shepherds would stone an ox if it gored a person to death, but its flesh would not be eaten and its owner wouldn't be punished (Exod 21:28–29). God also instructed his people how to treat the land. For example, if a fire broke out and spread, affecting standing grain or a field itself, the person who started it paid restitution (Exod 22:6). God's directives to Moses were made in order to establish a new religion and the structure of an evolving society.

Next, God redirected their attention away from their community and toward him. He told them not to mention the names of other gods. The Lord established national feasts and described how to set them up. Finally, he urged them to obey him and to avoid rebellion.

The Lord guided the Hebrews in attending to him. He listed gifts (e.g., gold and silver, and blue and scarlet material) to bring to him. The Hebrews built a sanctuary with a tabernacle. God instructed Hebrews to build the Ark of the Covenant with acacia wood overlaid with pure gold, including exact dimensions (Exod 25:10–11). Along with this construction, there were to be curtains of linen and goats' hair, boards, sockets, and a bronze altar, among other objects in the sanctuary. The Hebrews placed these artifacts within the court of the tabernacle. Consecrated priests (i.e., Aaron and his brothers) were directed to wear specific garments and have food prepared.[3] Essentially, God was establishing a new religion with all of its artifacts.

Finally, God listed the cost of the tabernacle. According to the website Bible History, the tabernacle had 2,800 pounds of gold, 9,600 pounds of silver, and 6,700 pounds of bronze.[4] This site explains that

---

3. Scores of instructions informed the faithful how to prepare each of these items.

4. In December 2020, the estimated cost of constructing the tabernacle would be $86.1 million.

gold represented the deity, silver stood for redemption, and bronze represented judgment.[5] The Hebrews erected the tabernacle, and God dwelled within it in the form of a cloud. This cloud occupied the tabernacle by day while a fire was present in it by night.

When?

Many dispute biblical details. People ask when events took place in Exodus. The website Bible Hub says that Exodus opens with Jacob's time in Egypt in 1800 BCE and Moses' birth 275 years later in 1525 BCE.[6] The book closes with the tabernacle being erected and filled with God's glory in 1445 BCE. From these dates, Exodus covers 355 years. Although Jacob starts the Exodus narrative in 1800 BCE, most of the story takes place between 1846 and 1845 BCE.

God placed ten plagues on the Egyptian people in 1446 BCE. These plagues helped to persuade the pharaoh to release the Hebrews from slavery. The Israelites started their flight from Egypt in 1446 BCE and moved to Mt. Sinai. It was here that they received the Ten Commandments, lost faith in Moses' claim of talking with God, and constructed a golden calf to replace the Lord.

The significance of the people's doubt in Moses was that it would lead to Moses loosing *legitimacy* with them. Thus, he would lose his authority over God's chosen people, and this emerging organized people would disintegrate into a mob.

During this same year, Moses received laws from God, and he prepared the tabernacle as the Lord's residence. In 1445 BCE, the Israelites completed the tabernacle, and the book of Exodus ends.

Where?

The entire Exodus story takes place in Egyptian territory and the wilderness to the southeast and east to Canaan (modern-day

---

5. Bible History, "Holy Materials."
6. Valkanet, "Bible Timeline."

Part III: First Five Books of the Bible

Israel), with twenty-three places noted. Maps 4.2 and 4.3 identify significant locations in Exodus.

Map 4.2: Siginificant Egyptian sites

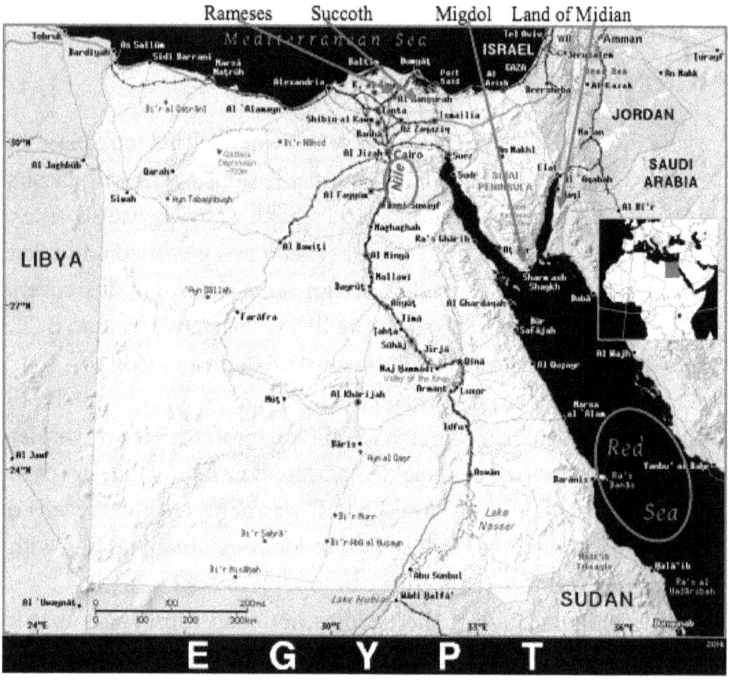

Source: Ian Macky, PAT

Exodus

Map 4.3: Mt. Sinai (Horeb); the Wildernesses of Shur, Sinai, and Sin; and Reuel (Edom)

Source: Ian Macky, PAT

The Exodus story begins in Egypt (see maps 4.2 and 4.3). It proceedes to Midian, where Moses escaped after he killed an Egyptian. Then, Moses led his people through the Red Sea and into the wilderness to wander for forty years. At this point, much of the story took place on and around Mt. Sinai.

We are not completely sure of many of the locations of the places named in Exodus. Therefore it is impossible to calculate distances among them accurately. However, one source claims the first thirty-nine years of wandering in the wilderness covered approximately 380 miles.[7] During the final year, Israelites covered 315 miles.[8] If these figures are accurate, God's chosen people wandered in the wilderness for forty years and covered 695 miles. Map 4.4 shows the Israelites' way from Egypt to Canaan's entrance.

7. Linker, "Wandering in the Desert."
8. McQueen and McQueen, "Mt. Sinai."

Part III: First Five Books of the Bible

Map 4.4: Israelites' Exodus from Egypt to the doorstep of Canaan

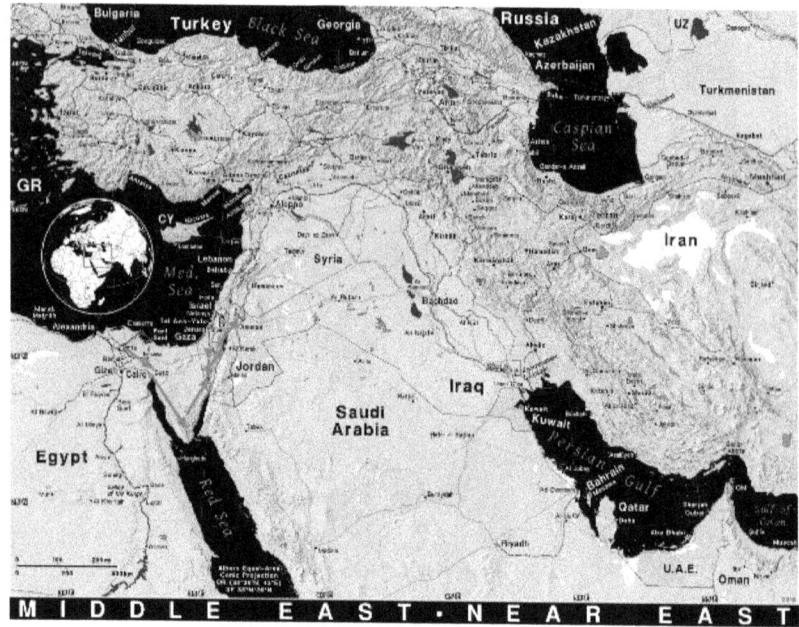

Source: Ian Macky, PAT

Why?

Genesis described the physical beginnings of God's people. Exodus marks their spiritual development. Hebrews agreed to take a singular God who commanded adoration from the people he saved. God formed a covenant with them that they would accept *only* him and he would bring them to a land of milk and honey (Canaan). Thus, Exodus is primarily a story about freedom (from slavery), establishing a monotheistic religion, and the birth of the nation of Israel.

How?

The word "exodus" means to exit or to migrate. The term suggests the book is about the Hebrews' escape from slavery in Egypt and their passage to the Promised Land. This narrative, however, takes up only a small portion of the text. The remaining sections compile rules—about 121 of them. These rules included directions for designing priests' garments, constructing the Ark of the Covenant with its tabernacle and sanctuary, and general ordinances and property laws. These rules give astonishingly detailed instructions. For instance, in Exodus 25:10–11, 33, God says:

> They shall construct an ark of acacia wood two and a half cubits long, and one and a half cubits wide, and one and a half cubits high. You shall overlay it with pure gold, inside and out you shall overlay it, and you shall make a gold molding around it.
>
> Three cups shall be shaped like almond blossoms in the one branch, a bulb, and a flower, and three cups shaped like almond blossoms in the other branch, a bulb, and a flower—so for six branches going out from the lampstand . . .

God continues His complicated directions:

> Moreover you shall make the tabernacle with ten curtains of the twisted linen and blue and purple and scarlet material, you shall make them with cherubim, the work of a skilled workman (Exod 26:1).
>
> The length of each curtain shall be twenty-eight cubits, and the width of each curtain four cubits; all the curtains shall have the same measurements (Exod 26:2).

Why did God speak with such specificity? Why was he so particular about the construction of the Ark of the Covenant and its related items, such as altars, curtains, and priestly garments? Curtains and priests' garments seem like such mundane items. Why would God of the universe bother himself with such detail? What kind of God demanded such exactitude?

How could this type of language be inspirational when God describes page after page, in agonizing detail, table construction, curtain-making, and lampstand assembly? For some, Exodus reads like a workman's manual more than an inspirational holy book.

CHAPTER 5

Leviticus

Who? What? When? Where? Why? How?

Summary of the Book of Leviticus

THE LEVITICUS STORY COVERS forty chapters and 859 verses and is shorter than the Genesis and Exodus epics. The word "Leviticus" relates to Levites, descendants of Levi, who was the son of Jacob and Leah. This book is replete with religious rules for the Levite priesthood. It holds 244 of the 613 commandments (about 40 percent) in the Bible's first five books. God gave these additional commandments to Moses, who communicated them to the Israelites in about 1400 BCE. Thus, Leviticus covers the events happening while the Israelites roamed the desert before entering the Promised Land.

At the end of Exodus, God descended from Mt. Sinai and entered the tent to meet with Moses. He gave detailed directions for how he wanted his ceremonies and rituals designed. In Leviticus 1–6, God describes the rituals attached to these offerings: burnt, grain, peace, sin, and guilt. The Hebrews who sinned were to make these offerings to God to gain his grace. These offerings did not include sacrificing humans, as did the rites of other groups at this time.[1] For instance, the burnt offering showed atonement in which priests would sacrifice an unblemished male animal, and they sprinkled the animal's blood around an altar.

Leviticus 6–7 describes how priests conducted ceremonies and rituals with each convention having these steps:

- Slay an animal.
- Sprinkle its blood around the altar.
- Offer an animal's tail, entrails, kidney, or liver fat.

Priests are to offer up these animal parts to God. Male priests should eat the remaining meat. Then God decrees dietary commandments, such as not eating dead animals' fat.

Leviticus 8 and 9, respectively, identify steps for consecrating priests and offering sacrifices. Moses consecrates Aaron and his sons first. Then they make sacrifices. Priests take at least twenty-five steps in these rituals, such as:

- Taking an animal (e.g., flawless, one-year-old calf, bull, ram, or goat),
- Burning it in the tent of meeting, and
- Congregants falling to the ground when smoke rises in reverence to the Lord as God's glory was evident to them.

Leviticus 10 tells the story of Nadab and Abihu, Aaron's sons, who light an unauthorized fire. Moses asks Mishael and Elzaphan, sons of Uzziel (Aaron's uncle), to take these guilty brothers out of the camp. God tells Eleazar and Ithamar (Aaron's other sons) to remain inside the tent. God kills Nadab and Abihu.

In Leviticus 11, the author returns to outlining ordinances with dietary regulations, such as which fish, birds, and insects to eat. Leviticus 12 cites social relationships, such as a woman remaining unclean for seven days after giving birth to a male. If it was a girl, she is "dirty" for two weeks.

---

1 Garrett, "5 Offerings."

Leviticus

Leviticus 13 and 14, respectively, outline a leprosy test and a law with twenty-three steps to clean a leper. If a man's wound is deep with infection and his hair in it is white, he has leprosy. A priest should direct someone to slay a bird and dip in its blood a live bird, cedar wood, scarlet string, and hyssop. Next, priests are given ten steps for cleaning a leper's house.

The author broadens the Lord's perspective in Leviticus 15 to include cleaning all types of unhealthiness. For instance, any bodily discharge, including seminal and menstrual discharges, is described as unclean. Unsanitary people remain impure for seven days until they wash and clean objects they touched. In Leviticus 16, forty ritual steps in the atonement process are detailed. After Aaron's sons die, priests prohibit Aaron from entering the holy place until he performs a cleansing ritual. Then God establishes an annual atonement event that takes place on the tenth day of the seventh month. This event eradicates sins committed during the year.

God directs the Israelites to worship only him and in his way by the tent of meeting (Lev 17–18). In Leviticus 19, God prohibits idolatry as the Lord asserts that he is the only true God and proclaims keeping the Sabbath holy.[2] Leviticus cites twenty-seven sundry laws. Six focus on agriculture and farming (e.g., do not breed two kinds of cattle together). Four relate to religious practices, such as not swearing in God's name. The remaining laws concentrate on social relations, such as not stealing or lying. Men who had sex with a slave would be punished but not put to death.

In Leviticus 20–22, God lays out rules prohibiting Israelites from pagan practices and describes regulations for priests, such as forbidding baldness. Leviticus 20 cites about thirteen sexual prohibitions, such as committing adultery and women having sex with animals. God cites laws for religious days (e.g., not working on the Sabbath). He commands ritual practices that include him receiving the first fruits from their harvest (Lev 23).

---

2. God tells the Israelites to practice the Sabbath and refrain from work on that day for seven times seven, or forty-nine, years, so they are to hold a Jubilee in the fiftieth year (Lev 25:8–13).

Part III: First Five Books of the Bible

Leviticus 24 covers several behaviors, like how to handle altar artifacts and how to treat murder and assault. A digression, however, occurs in chapter twenty-four. Shelomith, daughter of Dibri in the tribe of Dan, and her Egyptian husband have a son who fought with an Israelite man. Her son curses God, and Israelites stone him. The Lord asserts those who kill or injure another would likewise be killed or injured: "fracture for fracture, eye for an eye, and a tooth for a tooth" (Lev 24:20).

Leviticus 24–25 outlines community rights, which prohibit Israelites from permanently selling their land. If, however, a person could not reclaim his property, he could during the Jubilee year. Israelites could purchase pagan slaves and pass them down as possessions to their children. Fellow Israelites, however, are not to be treated this harshly. If they are too poor to buy their freedom, priests could release them during the Jubilee year. Finally, Israelites are to care for the poor among them.

In chapter twenty-six, the author returns to the theme of God's relationship with Israelites. If they obey him, he would bring rain for their crops, keep them in peace, and increase their population, among other blessings. Disobey him and God would make them sick, make their lands barren, and multiply their "agony seven times seven." He would unleash plagues and beasts, eat their children's flesh, and scatter them across nations. When they repent, he would save them from ultimate destruction because of his covenant with Jacob, Isaac, and Abraham.

Leviticus ends in chapter twenty-seven. God establishes punishments for those who reneg on their vows to him. The penalty depends on the value of the person or thing. For instance, a man or woman who is twenty to sixty years old and defaults on a vow to God should pay fifty shekels of silver if a man and thirty if a woman. If the vow includes an animal, house, or field, priests should adjust the punishment accordingly.

Leviticus

Who?

Genesis records over 300 individuals and groups, while Exodus had ninety-three individuals and sixteen groups. Leviticus has a paltry fifteen specified individuals, twelve categories of people (e.g., the poor and spiritualists), and two groups (i.e., the tribe of Dan and the Levites).

The sex composition of Leviticus, like previous books, is patriarchal. The book names twelve males and two females; Leviticus does not mention ages. Occupations, however, are cited. There are leaders (of the Israelites), priests (who were sons of Aaron), and mediums and spiritualists. *Stratification* shaped Egyptian and Israelite society alike. Additionally, Leviticus describes an agrarian society with farmers and vintners.

Extensive lists of families and their descendants were included earlier in the Bible. In Leviticus, however, the book cites only two families. The first reference is Aaron's sons (Nadab, Abihu, Eleazar, and Ithamar), his uncle (Uzziel), and his nephews (Mishael and Elzaphan) (Lev 10:1, 4, and 6). Next, the book mentions a fight between two boys. (Lev 24:10) One is the son an Israelite mother (Shelomith) and an Egyptian father.

Few characters occupy Leviticus. What is short in people, the book makes up for in the number of laws. The author infuses Leviticus with hundreds of God's directives, given to the Israelites through Moses.

What?

Genesis portrays the beginning of the human race and its near destruction and come back. Exodus described God's efforts that helped Moses and Aaron free the Israelites from slavery in Egypt, followed by God commanding them to be loyal to him. These books were grand in their stories. Leviticus narrows its focus to people, places, and performances. The cast of characters shrinks to fifteen individuals and two groups. The emphasis in Leviticus is on religious rules (norms) and priests who would implement them. Mt. Sinai is the only place cited. The Israelites received over 200 directives from God while living in a camp on the mountain. These decrees fall into three broad categories:

1. Agriculture,
2. Human Relationships, and
3. Religious Laws.

Each category contains an unequal number of laws. Agriculture had fourteen directives focused on farming and five on animal husbandry. Human relationships accounted for fifty-nine rules, such as dietary laws for health. Others concentrated on judges' conduct and laws governing loans, business, and the treatment of slaves. The largest category was religious laws. They covered sacrifices, tithes and offerings, and sinful relationships. Specific examples of each include:

Agriculture:

Do not crossbreed different species of animals (Lev 19:19).

Do not till the earth or sow the fields in the 7th year (Lev 25:4).

Human Relationships:

A judge must not show partiality to the rich . . . or poor (Lev 19:15).

Do not treat a Hebrew slave ruthlessly.(Lev 25:43).

Religious Commandments:

Do not sprinkle the blood of a blemished animal on the altar of God (Lev 22:19–24).

A man (Lev 15:13–15) or a woman (Lev 15:28–30) who has an abnormal discharge must bring a sacrifice.

Leviticus reads as if God, Moses, and the Levites sat on Mt. Sinai and designed policies and procedures for religious practices. The first six chapters of the book list laws covering burnt, grain, peace, sin, and guilt offerings. Later, the book contains laws

Leviticus

governing which animals to eat, motherhood, cleansing a leper, atonement, immoral relations, religious festivals, and redemption. Together, fourteen out of twenty-seven chapters (nearly 52 percent) present laws.

When?

Leviticus records no specific dates. However, the last verse, Moses receives the commandments from Mt. Sinai (Lev 27:34). Consequently, God communicated 244 rules recorded in Leviticus when the Israelites left Egypt and stayed on Mt. Sinai. According to Steve Rudd, a noted biblical commentator, the Israelites left Egypt and traveled twenty-four days to the Red Sea. Afterward, it took them another twenty days to reach Mt. Sinai. In total, from Egypt to Mt. Sinai, forty-four days transpired.[3] Then, the Hebrews camped for about one year on Mt. Sinai.[4] At the end of this time, the Israelites had completed the tabernacle. Their time on Mt. Sinai occurred in 1445 BCE, likely the year covered in Leviticus.

Looking beyond the Bible, humans used bronze from roughly 3300 to 1200 BCE. Thus, events in Leviticus occurred in the later stages of the Bronze Age.

Where?

Leviticus cites only one location: Mt. Sinai. God presents the Ten Commandments to Moses there; however, its location remains in doubt. Some locate it on the Sinai Peninsula, while others claim it is Mt. Horeb in Midian (Exod 3:1). This later location puts it in Saudi Arabia and not Egypt (See Map 5.1).

---

3. Rudd, "Exodus Route"
4. Orr, "Sinai."

Part III: First Five Books of the Bible

Map 5.1: Two locations of Mt. Sinai: Egypt and Midian

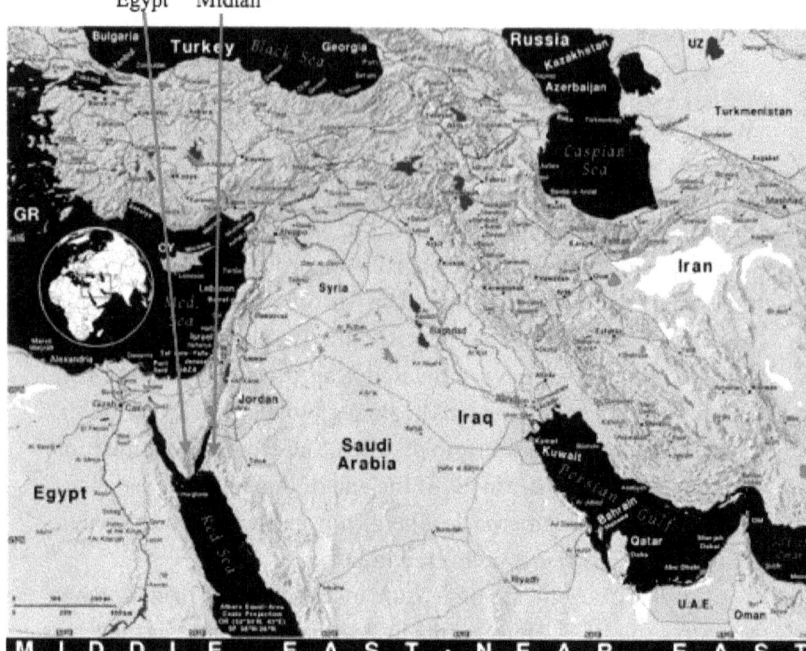

Source: Ian Macky, PAT

Why?

The tabernacle located inside the tent of meeting, only accessible by priests, was where God resided. The Israelites had completed the tent and tabernacle at the end of Exodus. The book of Leviticus gives laws and regulations for conduct within the tent, organized life in the camp, and sets out procedures for farming and husbandry. Leviticus is a rule book that gave an order to Hebrew life.

The rules follow this sequence:

1. Promulgated by God and given to Moses, then
2. Moses gave them to priests.

3. Priests passed them along to people.

These rules directed the sons of Israel:

1. How to behave appropriately toward one another.
2. How to get along in the desert's harsh environment.
3. How to worship God properly.

These were instructions for surviving socially, environmentally, and religiously.

How?

Exodus covered the construction of God's home on Earth with specific directions for assembling the tabernacle. In Leviticus, God gives Hebrews over 200 commandments on how to approach him. Additionally, God gave them directives on having healthy relationships, good hygiene, and eating correctly. These godly instructions helped the sons of Israel to survive in an unwelcoming desert environment. Examples follow:

> Do not fail to ritually purify by laundering and bathing at the appointed time after becoming ritually unclean (Lev17:16).
>
> A priest with a temporary blemish must not participate in the service until it has healed (Lev 21:18).
>
> A man must not have sexual relations with a woman betrothed to another man (Lev 19:20).
>
> Any clothing contaminated with a spreading disease is ritually unclean (Lev 13:47–59).
>
> Do not eat any unclean fish or seafood (Lev 11:10–12).

Through rules, laws, ordinances, and regulations, God fashioned Hebrew life. In sociological language, God was a functionalist because social order was his thing. God's attentiveness to social order was not surprising because the Israelites did not have an identity as a group. They were wandering in the desert,

Part III: First Five Books of the Bible

searching for food and water to survive. They lacked direction and found it in God through Moses and Aaron. The theme is that God saved them.

CHAPTER 6

Numbers

Who? What? When? Where? Why? How?

Summary of the Book of Numbers

THE FOURTH BOOK OF the Bible story is told in thirty-six chapters with 1,288 verses. It gets its name from including two main censuses. The story opens in the first month of the second year after the Hebrews left Egypt. They are still on Mt. Sinai. However, a group of new people have replaced the old generation and their details follow.

A census of Israel's (i.e., Jacob's) warriors records twelve tribes totaling 603,550 people (Num 1–2). This census, however, does not count Levite priests who guard the tent of meeting and tabernacle. Israel's population by tribe is listed Figure 6.1.

Part III: First Five Books of the Bible

Figure 6.1: Twelve tribes of Israel with their populations

Tribe	Number of Tribal Members
Reuben	46,500
Simeon	59,300
Judah	74,600
Issachar	54,400
Zebulun (Joseph's son)	57,400
Ephraim (Joseph's son)	40,500
Manasseh	32,200
Benjamin	35,400
Dan	62,700
Asher	41,500
Gad	45,650
Naphtali	53,400
	Total: 603,550

The Hebrews organize their camp around the tent of meeting based on the duties God outlines for each Israelite tribe who guarded each corner of the tent. For instance, Gershonites protect the tabernacle and tent, while Kohathites defend the sanctuary. The Gershonites and Kohathites were part of the tribe of the Levites.

A second census records the number of Levite priests. God wants to know how many of these priests are males of one month and older. There are 22,300 of them, but Aaron and Moses count 22,000 (Num 3:39). Then, God asks Moses and Aason to count the number of firstborns among the Israelites, which comes to 22,273. God places a ransom on the difference between the number of firstborn sons of warriors and the number of priests, that is, 273. Moses takes this amount of money and gives it to Aaron and his sons, as God demanded.

God asks for a third census in Numbers 4. He wants a count of Levi's sons' descendants: the Kohathites, Gershonites, Merarites, and Aaronites, who were thirty years of age and older. There were 17,160 of them. So, three censuses include warriors, priests, and the descendants of priests' families, which total 643,010 individuals.

Numbers

The story shifts to an account of Aaron and his sons. They are allowed entry into the tabernacle and sanctuary. If others entered, they die. When it is time to break camp, Aaron and his sons go into the tabernacle and sanctuary to prepare for travel. They cover the Ark of Testimony (that is, the Ark of the Covenant) with a veil. They perform at least fifteen other tasks. Then, the Kohathites prepare oil and holy objects for hauling. Next, the Gershonites take care of the tabernacle, tent, and the furnishings. Finally, the Merarites take the tabernacle and related articles.

Two topics dominate Numbers 5: camp cleanliness and an adultery test. First, God wants the camp to be clean because he resides there. Priests reject male and female lepers who discharge bodily fluids, such as semen, and priests banish them from camp. Second, wives who are suspected of committing adultery receive a test which consists of ingesting water. If she had committed adultery, her stomach would "swell and her thigh waste away" (Num 5:21–22). A woman achieves the freedom to have children if she passes the test.[1]

Numbers 6 presents the Law of the Nazirites, which establishes practices, penalties, and termination procedures for those who dedicated themselves to God. They promise not to drink wine, cut their hair, or go near a dead body. If they violate these restrictions, they are to shave their heads and bring turtledoves or pigeons to a priest who would sacrifice them in burnt and sin offerings.

Numbers 7–9 continues citing religious laws. Chapter seven notes that Moses established the tabernacle; the sons of Gershon and Merari donate carts and oxen; and Kohath do nothing because his people carry holy objects on their shoulders. Israelite leaders make offerings for twelve days. Chapter eight notes a ritual for cleansing Levites that included sprinkling purified water on themselves and removing their body hair. Priests offer grain, wave, sin, and burnt offerings, too. Instead of human sacrifices, God directs the Hebrews to offer their firstborn *ritually*. Lastly, God sets a Levite's priestly retirement at fifty years old. Chapter nine covers two

---

1. The adultery test recognizes the authority of a husband over his wife.

Part III: First Five Books of the Bible

issues: how to handle Passover when a man has been exposed to a dead body or traveled; and how to set up and tear down a camp.

Numbers 10 functions as a "how-to" manual for assembling a congregation, break camp, go to war, and begin a feast. Then the story shifts away from giving religious details to an account of time and place.

The sons of Israel make their first move from Mt. Sinai when the cloud (God) lifts from the tabernacle, and they leave the Sinai wilderness for the wilderness of Paran. This event happens on the twentieth day of the second month in the second year after leaving Egypt (Num 10:11–13). God details how the tribes should break camp and leave the mountain. Judah's people go first, followed by Merari's sons, who bring the tabernacle, and then the others. Reuel's son and Moses' father-in-law, Hobab, refuse to follow the tribes, and Moses warns him about disobeying God.

The Israelites' frustration with living conditions in the wilderness spill over into Numbers 11. They yearn for the plentiful food they'd had in Egypt. The complaints anger God. This places Moses between his suffering people and God's wrath. Moses' solution is to ask God to kill him. God calls upon Moses to assemble seventy elders at the tent of meeting. The Lord promises those who gathered that he will deliver more meat to the people than they could eat.

Moses' sister, Miriam, and brother, Aaron, speak out against Moses marrying a Cushite woman in Numbers 12. They also doubt his claim that he'd spoken to God. Then, God speaks to them and says he would communicate directly with Moses but with others through dreams. When God leaves, Miriam turns leprous; Aaron and Moses beg him to return her to health. The Lord says she will be healthy in seven days. It happens.

In Numbers 13, God directs Moses to send spies into Canaan to assess their strength and gather fruit. He sends scouts from Paran to the Valley of Eshcol where they gather the needed fruit. They proceede to the Zin Wilderness, which they report as land flowing with "milk and honey," having large and fortified cities, and housing populations of different people, such as Hittites and Jebusites.

Caleb (leader of the tribe of Judah) and Joshua (his father, Nun, originally in the tribe of Ephraim) want to rush in because they know God protects them, but others remain more cautious than these two (Num 14). God asks why they do not trust him, especially after he saved them in Egypt. God prophesizes that the non-believers (those who were more cautious) would spend forty years in the wilderness and die, while Joshua and Caleb would enter the Promised Land. Non-believers attack the Amalekites and Canaanites, but these groups (predictably) destroy them.

Numbers 15 focuses on unintentional and intentional sinning. God forgives those who give him offerings and banishes those who do not. Furthermore, those who successfully make it to Canaan have to give the Lord "thanksgiving" and "homage" with burnt and grain offerings. A side story about a man who cut wood on the Sabbath has God telling Moses to stone him. God then tells Moses to have Israelites wear tassels attached to a blue cord on each corner of their garments to remind them to keep God's commandments and be holy.

Two hundred and fifty congregational leaders rise against Moses and Aaron because they think the men placed themselves above the assembly and have failed to lead the Israelites into the Promised Land (Num 16:1–3). Moses calls on God, who opens the earth and swallows these rebellious kin along with their possessions. The next day, the Israelites are still disgruntled, so God brings a plague that kills 14,700 of them. He stops because Moses pleads with him to. Then, God directs Moses to collect a rod from each of the twelve Israelite houses and put them in the tent. The next day, Aaron's rod blossoms and becomes a reminder to the Israelites that they should not grumble before God.

Numbers 19 covers several procedures for things like touching a corpse or coming in contact with a bone or a grave. Each of these would make a person unclean for seven days. The section also describes how to make a person clean, which involves

Part III: First Five Books of the Bible

sacrificing a red heifer, spreading its blood, washing the person's clothing, and bathing one's body.

Miriam dies, so the Israelites bury her after arriving in the Zin Wilderness. The Israelites still grieve over their plight, so Moses takes it upon himself to chastise them. When God hears what he did, he reprimands Moses. Then the kings of Edom and Arad fight the Israelites who ask for and receive help from God. The Israelites set out from Mt. Hor by the Red Sea, circumventing the land of Edom. They continue to complain about their living conditions. When the Lord hears them, he sends fiery serpents, killing a number of them. Then, God feels sympathetic and wants to save them, so he tells Moses to make a bronze serpent and inform the people to look at it when snakes bite them. This bronze serpent would protect the people. Finally, Numbers records the Israelites' movement from camp to camp and the accounting of wars in the "book of wars."[2]

After the Israelites break camp, they head for the plains of Moab beyond the Jordan River and opposite Jericho. King Balak of Moab sees them coming, and he seeks an alliance with Balaam (a non-Israelite medium) to defeat the Israelites. However, God intervenes and convinces Balaam not to join Balak (Num 22–25).

Following a plague, God calls for two censuses: one of the warriors and another of priests.[3] Together there are 624,730 Hebrew males. Next, the Lord draws a formula for distributing land to these Israelites with larger groups getting more land than smaller ones. Finally, God kills all of those who left Egypt, except Caleb and Joshua (Num 26).

In Numbers 27–30, God resolves the problems of inheritance, succession, offerings, rituals, and vows.

1. Zelophehad died and has only two daughters. Should they receive his inheritance? God says, yes.

---

2. The book of wars records a poem that some say celebrated the Israelites' God-aided victories; among others, the defeats of Sihon, king of the Amorites, and Og, the Bashan king (Num 20–21).

3. The sons of Israel total 601,730 warriors. The House of Levi counts 23,000 priests.

2. Who should lead the Israelites after Moses' death? God ordains Joshua.

3. When do offerings take place? In the morning, at twilight, on the Sabbath, and at the beginning of each month. Passover occurs on the fourteenth day of the first month, while priests should hold feasts on the month's fifteenth day. On days one and seven, priests should hold convocations. The Lord prohibits working on these days, too.

4. Priests conduct rituals during the seventh month, and they hold offerings over eight days.

5. God says people should be true to their word and keep their vows. Husbands determine the faithfulness of husband-wife vows.

God commands the Israelites to war with Midianites in Numbers 31 and that they could take virgins and Midianite booty. However, the Israelites would be unclean if they touched any Midianite person or object and would have to conduct a cleansing ritual. God directs Hebrew warriors and priests to share Midianite treasure.

In Numbers 32, the tribes of Reuben and Gad, and later the tribe of Manasseh, want to settle west of the Jordan River. They do not want to enter the Promised Land because they have large livestock numbers that the Promised Land would not handle very well. However, Moses warns them that if they disobey God and do not enter the Promised Land, God would destroy them. Subsequently, they agree to fight for the Lord.

Numbers 33 presents a travelogue of forty-one places from Egypt through Mt. Sinai to the Jordan River banks where Israelites camped. God warns them to remove everyone and everything from the Promised Land; otherwise, they would become as "pricks in their eyes and thorns in their sides" (Num 33:55). Essentially, disobey the Lord and he will destroy non-believers and believers alike.

Numbers 34 answers three questions: What were Canaan's boundaries? Who apportioned the land? Who received its parcels? Canaan's boundaries were:

Part III: First Five Books of the Bible

- East from the Great Sea (Mediterranean) to Hazar-enan (a little northeast of Damascus).
- West from the Zin Wilderness to the Brook of Egypt and the sea.
- South from Hazar-enan to the Jordan River, ending at the Salt Sea (Dead Sea).

Land would be allocated by the priest Eleazar and Joshua (Nun's son). Family size determines allotment, with larger families getting more land than smaller ones. Reuben, Gad, and half of Manasseh's tribe would not enter Canaan. Thus, they do not receive parcels. Ten of twelve tribes of Israel receive land promised to them by God.

In Numbers 35, God gives a formula for distributing land on Canaan's outskirts to the Levites (priests). The Lord establishes forty-eight cities for them, of which God designates eight refuge cities. Next, God deals with the problem of murder by distinguishing between intended and unintended killings. If someone murders another, their punishment is death. A person who does not intend to kill another would be placed in a refuge city until its high priest died. A suspected murderer would have to be accused by more than one person.

The final problem, inheritance by marriage, is resolved in Numbers 36. God says a woman can marry anyone in her tribe, so the inheritance would remain with the group.

Who?

Numbers may be the most populated book of the Bible. This text contains five censuses, including two which are considered primary surveys.

In chapter 1, 603,550 Israelite warriors are in the census, while in chapter three, the author records 22,300 Levite priests. The total was 625,850. Three other censuses record subsets of Israelite warriors and Levite priests. For instance, also in chapter three, there are 22,273 firstborn males among the sons of Israel. There is a count of Levite priests thirty years of age and older in chapter four, but with no sums. In the same chapter, the number of Levite priests between thirty and fifty years old is 17,160.

Additionally, the author records 202 individuals and seventy-five groups. Among individuals cited, eight of them are females. The *patriarchal* bias of the Bible continues in its fourth book.

The three most prominent occupational statuses cited in Numbers are leaders of the Hebrew congregation, warriors, and priests. Ten leaders came from Jacob/Israel's sons: Reuben, Simeon, Judah, Issachar, Zebulun, Benjamin, Dan, Asher, Gad, and Naphtali. Two were Joseph's sons: Ephraim and Manasseh (Num 1:5-15). Each individual, twenty years of age or older and capable of going to war, is recorded by their family and individual names.

Priests came from the family of Levi, another one of Jacob/Israel's sons. Warriors came from the sons of Israel. They defended the chosen people, while the Levite priests took care of the tent of meeting, tabernacle, and paraphernalia. Priests began their holy duties at age twenty-five and retired at fifty years old. (Num 8:24-25).

In sociological terms, an occupational position in the religious structure was that of Nazirite (Num 6:1-21). Individuals in this position vowed dedication to God and to abstain from strong drink, among other restrictions. They went through a religious ceremony to acquire their status and to perform sacred roles.

Although not an occupation, another religious status was that of the layperson (Num 3:38). Congregants in this status participated in holy celebrations, but priests forbade them from entering the tent and viewing the tabernacle found within it. If they did either of these actions, the sanction was death.

Another non-occupational status was that of firstborn male, one month and older. God set their worth at five shekels. This money was an allowance given to Aaron and his priests for their living expenses (Num 3:40-51).

Numbers's author cites several ethnic groups (see Map 6.1). The Canaanites lived in the region known as Canaan or the Promised Land. The Jebusites lived south of the Amorites, and both of these groups resided west of the Canaanites. The Ammonites, Moabites, and Edomites dwelled east of the Jordan River and the Salt Sea (Dead Sea).

Part III: First Five Books of the Bible

Map 6.1: Seven of the ethnic groups

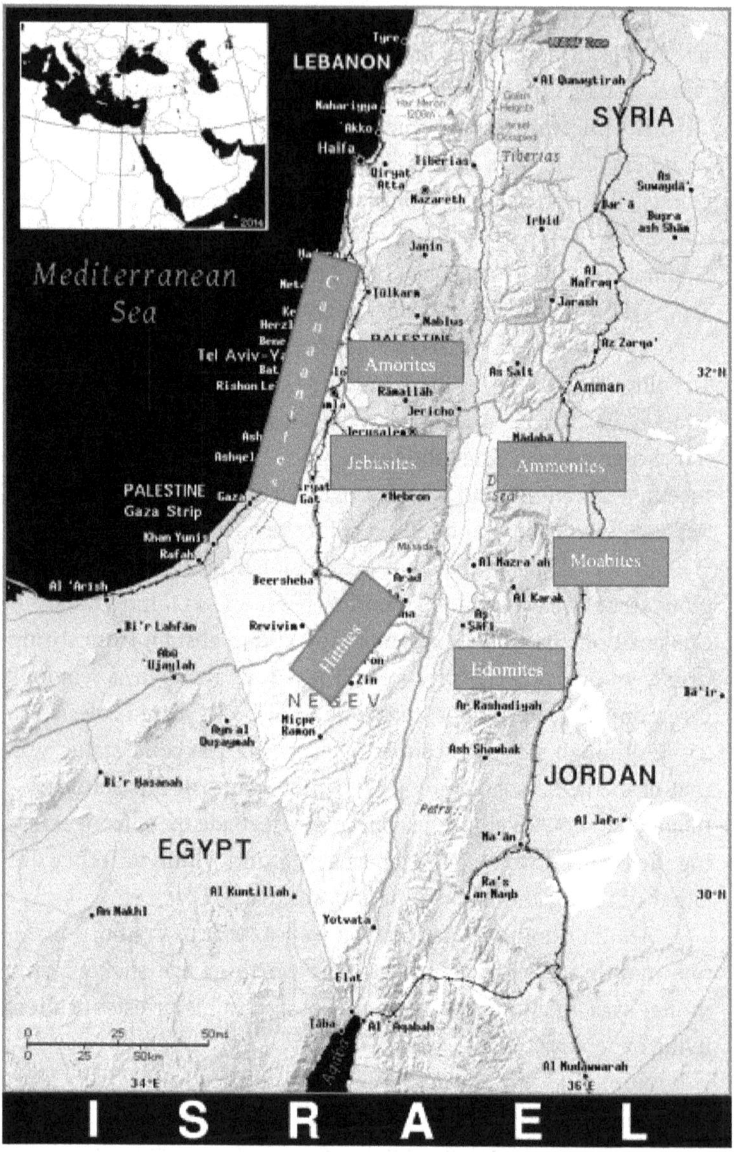

Source: Ian Macky, PAT

Numbers

Additionally, Miriam and Aaron were upset with Moses, who married a Cushite woman (Num 12:1), and someone slew a Midianite woman because she had relations with an Israelite man (Num 25:14).

What?

Numbers's first census counted 603,550 Israelite warriors. Its second census listed 601,730 first-generation people who did not come from Egypt. Although this book records population surveys, it is not only about figures.

Israelites' camp organization and priests' duties appeared in earlier chapters. The families of Dan, Reuben, Judah, and Ephraim guarded the north, south, east, and west sides of the tent of meeting, respectively. The Levite priesthood was made up of the descendants of Levi's sons: Gershon, Kohath, and Merari. Each family was assigned specific priestly duties, such as caring for the tent and tabernacle (Gershonites), looking after the sanctuary (Kohathites), and maintaining tabernacle paraphernalia like pillars and sockets (Mahlites). These arrangements demonstrated that the Israelites had a *division of labor* that organized their society and indicated that they were developing a complex society.

Religious ceremonies, such as Passover, are described along with accompanying artifacts, such as trumpets and lampstands. Priests held Passover on the fourteenth day of the month at twilight (Num 9:3). Numbers's author gives detailed descriptions of offerings and sprinkles their timing throughout the text. Numbers records the death of significant people, such as Miriam and Aaron, as well as Hebrew laws concerning:

1. Sojourners, share with them (Num 15:15);
2. Sabbath-breakers, put them to death (Num 15:35);
3. Surviving daughters, receive inheritance, if there were no sons (Num 27:8); and
4. Vow-makers, do not violate your word (Num 30:2).

Next, God directs the Israelites to slaughter Midianites who occupied land promised to them. Additionally, the Lord told Moses to inform the Hebrews that Joshua would lead them into the Promised Land after Moses died.

In Exodus and Leviticus, God gave the Hebrews commands, while in Numbers, they leave the wilderness and ready themselves to enter the Promised Land.

When?

Numbers 1:1 states:
"Then the Lord spoke to Moses in the wilderness of Sinai ... on the first of the second month, in the *second year after* [emphasis added] they had come out of the land of Egypt ..."

The book ends with
"... in the plains of Moab by the Jordan opposite Jericho" (Num 36:13).

At the end of the book, the Israelites are about to enter the Promised Land. If they left Egypt about 1447 BCE and God spoke to Moses on Mt. Sinai around 1445 BCE, and they arrived at the doorstep of the Promised Land on the Plains of Moab thirty-eight years later in about 1407 BCE. This timeframe covered the forty years the Israelites wandered in the desert.

Where?

Most of Numbers's events take place in the wilderness east of Egypt and southwest of Canaan. Generally, they happened in the wildernesses of Sinai and Sin (see Map 6.2). Specifically, in chapter thirty-three, a veritable travelogue of approximately forty-two places of the Israelite journey from Egypt to the Jordan River are recorded (Num 33:3–48). They went from: Rameses—Succoth—Almon-Diblathaim (in the Abarim Mountains before Nebo)—the plains of Moab (by the Jordan, opposite Jericho; from Beth-Jeshimoth as far as Abel-Shittim in the plains of Moab).

Numbers

Map 6.2: Journey (blue arrows) **through the wilderness**

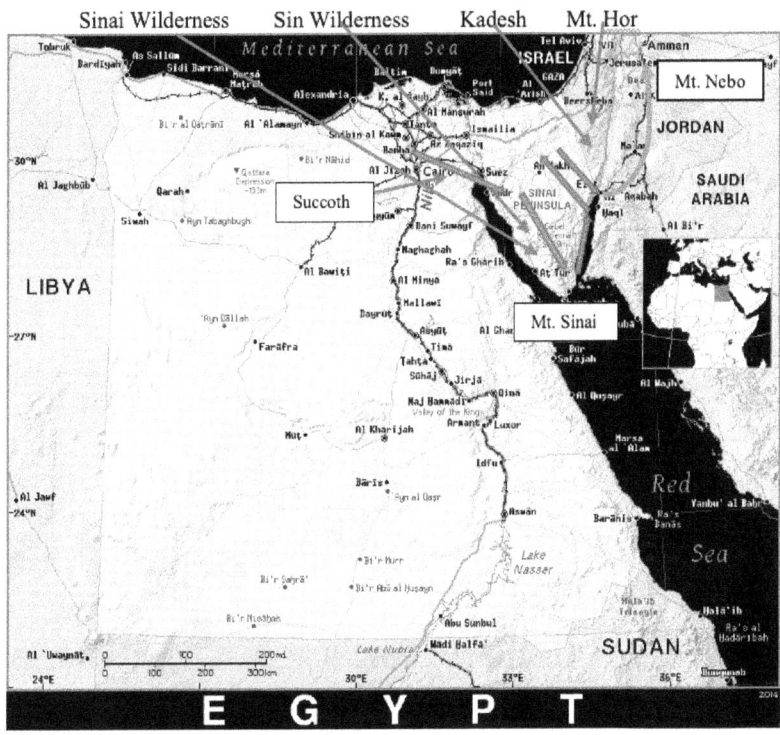

Source: Ian Macky, PAT

Where was the Promised Land, then? According to Genesis 15:18, "The Lord made a covenant with Abram, saying, 'To your descendants, I have given this land, from the *river of Egypt* as far as the great river, the *river Euphrates*. . .'" (Italics added; see Map 6.3).

Part III: First Five Books of the Bible

Map 6.3: Promised Land boundaries according to Genesis

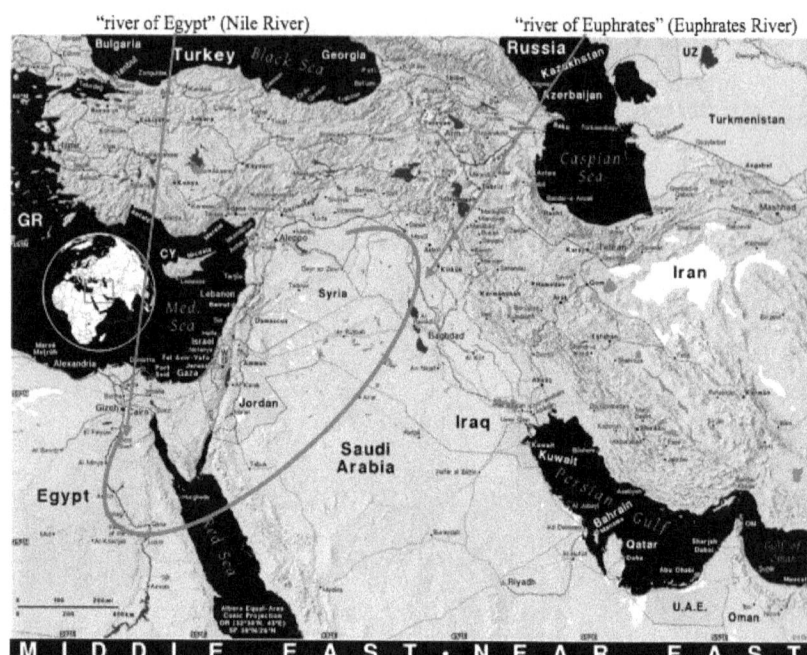

Source: Ian Macky, PAT

Numbers 34:2–12, however, states these boundaries as (See also Map 6.4):

> ... the land of Canaan borders ... southern section from the Zin Wilderness by Edom, the southern border from the end of the Salt Sea eastward, and turn south to the top of Akrabbim. Continue to Zin, and end south of Kadesh–barnea. Reach Hazaraddar and continue to Azmon to the brook of Egypt, and end by the sea.
> ... the western border from the Great Sea and its coastline ...
> ... north border from the Great Sea to Mt. Hor to the Lebo-hamath, and terminate at Zedad. Then proceed to Ziphron and terminate at Hazar–enan ...
> ... eastern border draw a line from Hazar-enan to Shepham and go down to Riblah on the east side of Ain.

Numbers

Then go down and reach the slope on the east side of the Sea of Chinnereth, and go down to the Jordan. End at the Salt Sea.

Map 6.4: Promised Land boundaries according to Numbers

Source: https://ian.macky.net/pat/map/il/il_blk.gif

Where, then, is the Promised Land? Does it extend to the Euphrates River, as stated in Genesis, or is Mt. Hor its northern border, as Numbers claimed?

Why?

The book of Numbers is the end of the beginning. Genesis recorded Creation, while Exodus and Leviticus documented laws dictated by God to Moses. By the time of Numbers, people found initially in earlier books of the Bible either died of natural causes

Part III: First Five Books of the Bible

or were about to be killed by God for disobeying him. According to Numbers 32:11–13:

> None of the men who came up from Egypt, from twenty years old and upward, shall see the land which I swore to Abraham, to Isaac, and to Jacob; for they did not follow Me fully[4] ... [except Caleb and Joshua] ... So the Lord's anger burned against Israel, and He made them wander in the wilderness forty years, until the entire generation of those who had done evil in the sight of the Lord was destroyed.

Thus, a new generation was about to enter the Promised Land. In a new land promised to God's chosen people, a fresh start with God was about to begin.

How?

The title of the fourth book of the Bible indicates readers would see lots of statistics, and this is the case. Statistics, among others, record the number of:

1. Refuge cities: six (Num 35);
2. Days Israelite leaders gave offerings to the Lord: twelve (Num 7);
3. Israelite warriors in the camp: 603,500 (Num 2);
4. Levite males, one month and older: 22,000[5] (Num 3:39);
5. Sons of Israel, firstborn, one month and older: 22,273 (Num 3:43);

---

4. God would kill everyone who came from Egypt. They doubted the Lord. Only Caleb and Joshua would enter the Promised Land because they believed God would protect them against the Hebrews' enemies.

5. The number of Levite men by their families who were male and one month old and older was 22,000. However, by a manual count of them, as presented in Numbers 3:22, 28, and 34, there were 22,300. I guess Moses had as much trouble counting as do I.

6. Sons/families of Levi; thirty to fifty years old: 17,160 (Num 4:34–48);

7. Census of new generation of Sons of Israel, twenty years and older: 601,730 (Num 26:1–51);

8. People who complained and God killed by the plague: 14,700 (Num 16:49); and

9. Midianite booty to be divided: 675,000 sheep; 72,000 cattle; 61,000 donkeys; and 32,000 humans (Num 31:32–35).

Was God "figuring" out how many men were eligible for an army to conquer the Promised Land? Was he determining who was qualified for service in the priesthood after arriving in the Promised Land? The Lord counted the disobedient, killing the deviant. Finally, he tallied the number who would occupy the land and computed available goods (especially booty) for them. Essentially, he planned how to conquer the land and how to sustain people once they got there.

CHAPTER 7

Deuteronomy

Who? What? When? Where? Why? How?

Summary of the Book of Deuteronomy

THE BIBLE'S FIFTH BOOK, Deuteronomy, has thirty-four chapters and 959 verses, and it completes the Jewish Torah and the Christian Pentateuch. "Deuteronomy" means the repetition of the law. Moses was dying and preparing himself for a journey to heaven. Before going, however, he repeated laws and events important in his life. Moses implored the Israelites to obey God's laws, so he repeated them again, again, and again.

Moreover, the book recounts their tumultuous journey from Egypt to the Promised Land. Deuteronomy's early chapters read like a travelogue and history book. They report places Hebrews passed on their way to the Promised Land and identified groups who, past and present (in the world of the Bible), occupied these lands.

In Deuteronomy 1, Moses speaks on the banks of the Jordan River in Moab. He reminds the Israelites that the land across the river was promised to them by God. They were, however, leery about crossing this river, fearing the people living on the other side, who were bigger and taller than Hebrews and lived in fortified cities. A source identifies this region as the land of Rephaim (giants). God directs spies to be sent into Rephaim to assess their strength. Still, the Israelites do not cross the Jordan, which angers God. He vows that no one originally from Egypt, except Caleb and Joshua, would enter the Promised Land.

As Moses speaks in Deuteronomy 2, he repeats previous stories, such as leaving Egypt, wandering in the desert, and traveling through hostile territory. He recounts Hebrew victories, booty collected, and lands captured by them.

Deuteronomy 3 tells how, with God's help, Hebrews defeated kings Og and Sihon and took their men, women, children, possessions, and sixty cities. It explains how the Israelites divided this booty and finishes with Moses' plea to enter the Promised Land and God's denial of his request.

Deuteronomy 4–6 covers God's laws again. Moses says God's wrath has fallen on those who disobeyed his laws. He reminds them of their covenant with God that includes the Ten Commandments. Next, Moses states that God has led them out of Egypt to be his possession. He explains why God has prohibited him from entering the Promised Land: Moses took it upon himself to save the Hebrews; consequently, he did not trust the Lord. Next, the author restates Canaan's boundary lines. Moses reminds the Hebrews that God is fierce and forgiving. Which side of God they would experience depended on whether they obeyed or disobeyed him. Finally, God establishes three cities on the Jordan's east side as places of refuge for those accused of manslaughter.

Deuteronomy repeats the content previously mentioned. In chapter seven, God recounts his wish for the Israelites to destroy everyone occupying the Promised Land, his prohibition on intermarriage with these inhabitants, and his demand that their holy places and objects be obliterated. In return, God would love and protect them, defeat their adversaries, provide them with sustaining commodities (e.g., fruit, wine, and oil), and allow them to propagate. In short, God would bless them over all others.

Why did the Israelites wander in the desert for forty years? (Deut 8) God says it was a test to see what was in their hearts, making them humble and tough. If they adhered to God's commandments, their population would grow, and they would retain their land. Disobey his commandments and they would perish. To reduce Hebrew snobbery, God reminds them of earlier transgressions against him, such as their rebellion at Mt. Sinai and creating a molten calf to replace him (Deut 9).

Moses provides a detailed retelling of his second ascension on Mt. Sinai to receive God's second set of commandments. Moses rhetorically asks the Hebrews what they must do, and answers with keeping God's commandments and fear, love, and serve him. Next, Moses describes God's attributes: great, mighty, awesome, fair, loving, and God of gods (Deut. 10–11).

In Deuteronomy 12–14, Moses reiterates Israel's need to heed God's laws or suffer personal and national extinction. He warns them not to follow false gods. He pronounces God's laws that distinguish between water and land creatures and which among these one could eat.

Chapters 15–16 discuss the sabbatical year and various feasts. A sabbatical occurs every seven years when the Hebrews are to be generous, forgive debts, and free Hebrew slaves. This section discusseds feasts, too. Passover is the Feast of Unleavened Bread celebrated in the month of Abib in commemoration of leaving Egypt. The Feast of Weeks starts seven weeks after harvesting grain. Again, it observes the Hebrews' exit from Egypt. The Feast of Booths, held three times per year, is to be convened seven days after collecting grain and filling the wine vat. Lastly, Moses implores the Israelites to pursue justice, be impartial, and not assume god-like status.

The administration of justice; assistance for Levite priests; laws for giving testimony and conducting warfare properly; and guidelines for a rebellious and stubborn son are covered in Deuteronomy 17–21. For instance, the Israelites are encouraged by Moses neither to present the Lord with blemished oxen or sheep nor to follow those who served other gods. Doing so is not merely bad behavior, but it means death.

Deuteronomy

Although Levite priests would not receive inheritances, they can collect meat, grain, new wine, and other commodities. Proper prescriptions for giving testimony include:

- Two or more witnesses, not one;
- No false witnessing;
- Giving a "life for life, eye for an eye, tooth for tooth, hand for hand, foot for foot" (Deut 19:21); and
- Not pitying a false accuser.

Rules of warfare include offering peace to enemy cities. If they refused, then they could be killed. Distant cities' booty is available to Hebrews, and in captured areas, they are to obliterate god-worshipping. Hebrews should appoint commanders, and priests should give "pep talks" to the warriors. The Israelites are reminded that God has protected them. This message would be vital when enemy armies were bigger and stronger than them. Some soldiers are to be exempt from battle, including those:

- Building a new house,
- Planting a vineyard,
- Engaged to a woman, or
- Who remained fainthearted.

Hebrew warriors could marry captured women. These women could shave their heads, trim their nails, and mourn their mothers and fathers for one month. If these captured wives displeased their husbands, their husbands could dismiss them. But husbands could neither sell nor mistreat their wives. Finally, a rebellious and stubborn son could be stoned to death by city elders.

Deuteronomy 22–25 cites a variety of laws that cover morality and divorce, among other areas. One law states that the Hebrew community would kill a man who raped a girl. A divorced man could not remarry his remarried first wife because her second husband defiled her. No one could oppress hired men, most notably poor ones. More mundane rules include:

Part III: First Five Books of the Bible

- People had to bury excrement outside a camp,
- Men emitting nocturnal emissions must leave camp until they bathed,
- Foreigners could be charged interest but not countrymen, and
- The community ban having two sets of weights and measures.

In Deuteronomy 26, Moses informs the Israelites to take their first harvest to the Lord, with the third year being the Year of Tithing. Then, in the Curses of Mt. Ebal, Moses tells the Israelites to take Mt. Ebal's large stones and write down God's laws using lime. Next, Moses distinguishes between the blessed from those who violate God's laws (i.e., cursed) (Deut 27). The holy were Simeon, Levi, Judah, Joseph, and Benjamin, while the cursed were Reuben, Gad, Asher, Zebulun, Dan, and Naphtali.

Most of Deuteronomy 28 lists consequences for disobeying God's commandments. A horrible litany of punishments ensues, such as descriptions of the Promised Land turning barren and God destroying all generations of the Hebrews. The Promised Land would be verdant and populated with healthy and prosperous Hebrews. Deuteronomy 30 returns to this theme. Moses reminds the Israelites to choose life, which means keeping God's commandments so they would not perish. In Deuteronomy 29, Moses again recounts the story of the Hebrews in Egypt, forty years of wandering in the desert, and Hebrew battles against kings Sihon and Og.

Chapters 31–34 focuses on endings. In Deuteronomy 31, Moses gives his last counsel. He is 120 years old. He tells the Hebrews to be courageous because God is with them. In Deuteronomy 32, God provides a song to Moses. The Lord wants it sung throughout the ages. He directs Moses to call Joshua to him. The Lord commissions him as the leader of the Hebrews after Moses' death. Then God tells Moses to ascend Mt. Nebo in Moab's Abarim Mountains opposite Jericho. Moses looks over Canaan and dies.

Although the biblical narrative puts Moses' death in Deuteronomy 32, Moses continues to speak in Deuteronomy 33. He recounts places where God gave commandments and blessed Israel's tribes. Then Moses' death site, as stated in Deuteronomy

Deuteronomy

32, is restated in Deuteronomy 34. Next, Joshua leads the chosen people across the Jordan River into the land promised to them by God as far back as the time of Jacob (Israel), Isaac, and Abraham. Thus ended are the first five books of the Bible.

Map 7.1 shows the location of the Hebrew tribes in and around the Promised Land.

Map 7.1: Tribes inside and outside (Reuben, Gad, and half of Manasseh) the Promised Land—Twelve tribes of Israel

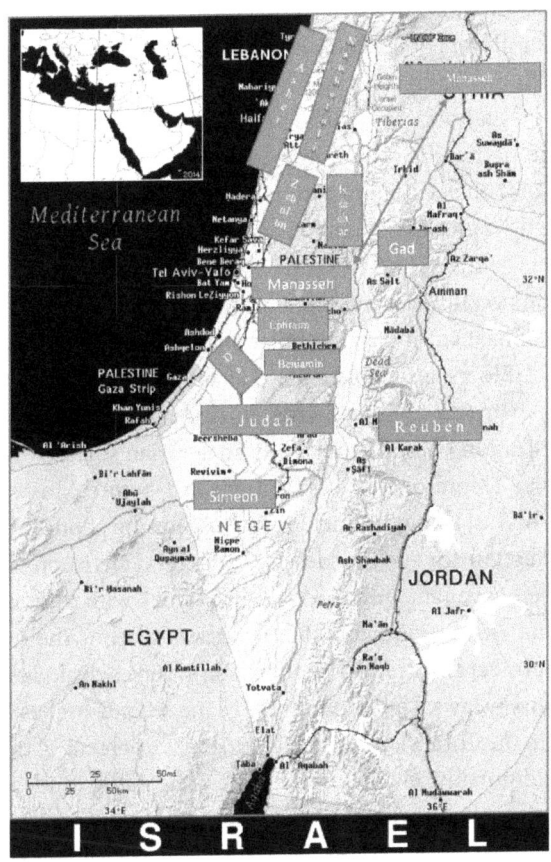

Source: Ian Macky, PAT

Part III: First Five Books of the Bible

Who?

Deuteronomy does not mention many new people; however, several are repeated from earlier texts. Not having new people in the book is not surprising since Moses reminisces about important themes, events, and people who wandered with him in the desert for forty years.

Individuals (forty-one) and groups (forty-three), nearly evenly divided in numbers, are recorded. Individuals mentioned are major players of the Bible, such as Moses, Abraham, Isaac, and Jacob. The Rephaim (Canaan's giants) and Avvim (indigenous living near Gaza) occupy Canaan before the Hebrews.

The patriarchal structure of the Bible continues in Deuteronomy and the sex composition remains imbalanced. The book cites vastly more males than females. The only females named are Asherim (goddess) and Miriam (Moses' sister).

Additionally, the inclusion of two kings, Sihon of Heshbon and Og of Bashan, and an Egyptian pharaoh, suggest a hierarchical structure. Elders, also, hold a place of authority while people listen to their instruction. Since herds, flocks, and shepherds populate this civilization, these factors imply an agrarian society.

Since Deuteronomy covers time just before Moses died, it records his last thoughts, including those for the people he had the most affection for—fellow desert wanderers. He impresses upon them their covenant with God and also struck with their founders: Abraham, Isaac, and Jacob. Simply, it was to obey the Lord, and he will protect them. Most Deuteronomy verses deal with norms, most notably laws. Deuteronomy cites the second-highest number of laws in the Torah/Pentateuch (197, or 32.1 percent of the total).[1]

Additionally, chapter seven lists pre-existing and concomitant ethnic groups who occupy Canaan when the Hebrews reach the Jordan River. They are the Hittites, Girgashites, Amorites, Canaanites, Perizzites, Hivites, and Jebusites. God directs the Hebrews to destroy them and to take their land.

---

1. Leviticus has most laws, with 242 or 39.5 percent of the total.

Statuses, such as husbands, wives, fathers, mothers, and priests, define Hebrew society. These foretold institutions of marriage, family, and religion in Hebrew society. Although the Bible previously mentioned these social arrangements, now they describe Hebrew social structures. The Israelites were organizing into a society, shifting from mostly a wandering, unorganized people into an organized group about to settle the Promised Land. This land had cities and social structures, such as institutions.

What?

Deuteronomy was Moses' swan song, where he records his last words before the Hebrews would enter the Promised Land. A dying person does not speak about trivialities, so Moses' words were of utmost importance.

He spoke about God's laws and told the Hebrews to keep the Lord's commandments or perish. These laws organized individual and group behavior. They managed people's behavior within religious, judicial, and familial institutions. Moses made a serious effort to structure Hebrew life around God's directives.

When?

Deuteronomy records: "In the fortieth year, on the first day of the eleventh month, Moses spoke to the children of Israel..." (Deut 1:3).

Moses and the chosen people were in the last days of wandering in the desert and on the cusp of entering the Promised Land. At the end of Deuteronomy, when Moses dies, the Israelites are ready to cross the Jordan River, 400 years after God promised Abraham this territory.

The first five books of the Bible (i.e., Torah/Pentateuch) cover time from its beginning (4004 BCE) to Moses' death (1405 BCE), which was just before the Israelites entered the Promised Land. Thus, this epic story covers almost 2,600 years.

Part III: First Five Books of the Bible

Where?

Where was Moses when he spoke in Deuteronomy? He was east of the Jordan River in the wilderness,

> ... in the Arabah opposite Suph [Red Sea] between Paran and Tophel and Laban and Haze Roth and Dizahab. It is 11 days' journey from Horeb by way of Mt. Seir to Kadesh-barna (Deut 1:1–2).

Thus, Moses moved his people from the northeast of Mt. Sinai (Horeb) northward to Kadesh–barna. Then he moved, once more, eastward to the Land of Moab on the east side of the Jordan River. Moses' resting place is on top of Mt. Nebo on the east side of the Dead Sea.

Map 7.2 shows the journey that took the Hebrews to the edge of the Promised Land.

Map 7.2: From Mt. Sinai to Mt. Nebo—Moses' last journey

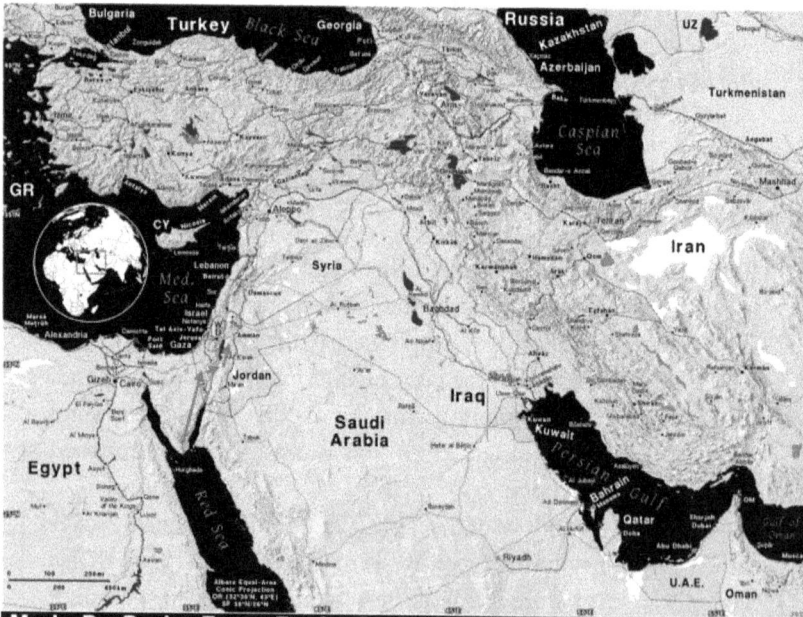

Source: Ian Macky, PAT

Why?

For Jews, Deuteronomy ends the Torah (first five books of the Bible), and these books are extremely holy because God spoke directly to them through Moses.[2]

Deuteronomy also was the last book in which Moses spoke, and in it, he has two topics that preoccupy him. First, Moses knows he would not enter the Promised Land, but he wants to prepare those who would.[3] Second, Moses knows death is imminent. As he faces eternity, he shares his life lessons with his followers. Both these concerns focus on the same topic: God's laws. Moses knows the Hebrews would thrive in the Promised Land if they obey the Lord's directions. Therefore, Moses wants to make sure they know what God demands of them. He also wants them to retain God's laws, so he repeats and repeats them.

How?

"Deuteronomy" means "second law."[4] It is *not* a first and second law, such as the first and second law of thermodynamics. It indicated there was a second rendition of God's laws. The Bible elucidated these laws earlier and repeats them as if to drum them into the Israelites' minds. God, through Moses, repeats these laws in Deuteronomy to indicate their extreme importance. Obey God's laws and prosper in the Promised Land. Disobey them, and God will destroy Hebrew civilization and kill the Israelites. Thus, deviance from God's laws leads to extreme negative sanctions.

---

2. Schechter, "Deuteronomy."

3. God told Moses to talk to a rock, not strike it, and get water for Hebrews (Deut 32:51–52). Since Moses disobeyed God, he was prohibited entry into the Promised Land.

4. Orr, "Deuteronomy."

PART IV

Commentary on the First Five Books of the Bible

CHAPTER 8

Observations on the Torah/Pentateuch[1]

Introduction

FOR JEWS, THE TORAH is the word of God. For Christians, the Pentateuch provides a foundation of belief that is materialized in the life of Jesus, who appears later in the Bible. For Jews, the Torah holds 613 commandments. For Christians, the Ten Commandments found in Exodus represent God's directives to humans. The Torah/Pentateuch is the first five books of the Bible: Genesis, Exodus, Leviticus, Numbers, and Deuteronomy, which constitutes 187 chapters with 5,852 verses (see Figure 8.1).[2]

Figure 8.1: The first five books of the Bible

Bible books	No. of chapters	No. of verses
Genesis	50	1,533
Exodus	40	1,213
Leviticus	27	859
Numbers	36	1,288
Deuteronomy	34	959
Totals:	187	5,852

1. This section does not present an authoritative interpretation of the Torah/Pentateuch. I do not claim to be a theologian.

2. Multiple sources cite the Bible with 1,189 chapters and 31,102 verses. Therefore, the first five books of the Bible contain about 15.5 percent of the Bible's chapters and almost 19 percent of its verses.

Part IV: Commentary on the First Five Books of the Bible

Leviticus 12:1-8 has the fewest lines. Eight verses discuss purification procedures for mothers after they give birth to male and female children. The greatest number of verses were found in Numbers 7:1-89. This chapter outlines how leaders should give offerings to God.

The first five books of the Bible cite thousands of people. Specifically-named individuals are plentiful but undoubtedly far fewer than the thousands of unnamed people (see Figure 8.2).

Figure 8.2: Individuals named in the first five Bible books

	Genesis	Exodus	Leviticus	Numbers	Deuteronomy
No. of identified names	316	71	14	195	32
Percentage of females	8 percent	4 percent	0 percent	3.6 percent	3 percent

Readers, however, must be careful with these numbers. Are 628 individual people named in these books?[3] These books repeat many names. Sometimes this occurs within one book, while at other times they are retold in different books. For instance, Anah appeared in Genesis at least three times (Gen 36:20, 24, and 29). It is unclear if Anah is the same or a different individual in each of these passages. Genesis, Exodus, Leviticus, and Deuteronomy cite Abraham, so adding his name each time would yield a false total since he is the same person.

Interestingly, males overwhelmingly populate these books. As Figure 8.2 shows, Genesis holds the largest percentage (eight) of named females in a book. This sex ratio means twenty-five out of 316 people named in Genesis are females.[4] This sparse distribution by sex indicates the patriarchal character of these texts.

---

3. This 628 figure represents the total number of identified names in Torah/Pentateuch.

4. The phrase stated throughout the Bible, ". . . and he had other sons and daughters" indicates many more females resided among the chosen people than are cited explicitly in the text.

Observations on the Torah/Pentateuch

Genesis

The first words of the Bible are "*In* the beginning." Why didn't the book start with "*At* the beginning?" According to the Cambridge English Dictionary, when 'at' is used as a preposition of time, it is definite. When 'in' is employed as a preposition of time, it is less specific. So God, or the author of Genesis, was purposefully vague about when Creation began.

Then, the author takes over fifty chapters with approximately thirty stories to detail Creation. First, the story describes the physical world, and later it tells of the people who populate it. Remarkably, when these stories fill a person, one's consciousness comes to perceive the entire world as constituting only these people, places, and events. One comes to sense others (e.g., Hittites, Indus Valley Indians, and Chinese) either do not exist or are of such unimportance they do not merit recognition in the Bible. At best, groups like these provide a backdrop to people God chooses as belonging to him.

Scientists claim the universe began about thirteen billion years ago. According to the Bible, however, God created the universe in six days and rested on the seventh day (Gen 1:1–31). Furthermore, many biblical specialists fix the beginning in 4004 BCE. Consequently, scientific and biblical researchers have a difference in the length of time it took for the cosmos to form, and when it started.

When did God create Adam and Eve? Genesis 1:26 states, "Then God said, 'Let Us make man in Our image, according to Our likeness....'"[5] Genesis 2:7 says, "Then the Lord formed man of dust from the ground, and breathed into his nostrils the breath of life, and man became a living being."

When did God create man? Was it on day six of Creation, as stated in chapter one, or later, as recorded in chapter two? Why did God announce the creation of man in two chapters? Did God reiterate in chapter two what he created in chapter one? Is it only an

---

5. What does "our" mean in Genesis 2:7? To whom is God referring? Is he employing the "royal" our, or are there other gods around him?

Part IV: Commentary on the First Five Books of the Bible

error in writing by the author, or is it meant to confuse or frustrate readers? Could it be the author's point to tell us something about the nature of life? Did the author inform us that contradiction is at our core? Was he saying the essence of man and the world was contradictory? Was the author asserting life's complexity?

We ponder these lines, but no simple answers emerge. We fret over them. We pursue answers while little is given to us by the author. We can create a response, remain ignorant, or listen to the deity who spoke to us through these tracts. The story told in the Bible moves its readers to select its message to obey God and inherit the Promised Land.

Another interpretation, however, comes to mind. Perhaps passages in Genesis call humankind to assume responsibility for itself—construct and create answers for life's intricacies. Bible believers may see this interpretation as arrogant and blasphemous. They view this position as man, not God, creating answers, as if this response somehow negates God. However, possibly, humanity may arrive at answers through humbly seeking out a spiritual thread running within them. That is, people search within them, at their core, for the divine.[6] In any case, I will remain faithful to the Bible's interpretation in this book.

The author structures the Genesis story around a cast of characters, events, and sub-plots. Its main characters are: Adam and Eve, Noah, Abraham, Isaac, Jacob/Israel, and Joseph (See Figure 8.3 below).

---

6. What if believers and non-believers are *both* correct? How? Aren't these positions contradictory? According to biblical texts, God created everyone, and he loves all of us, believers and non-believers. If both types of people are true to themselves, and God loves everyone, aren't all people embraced within his arms?!

Observations on the Torah/Pentateuch

Figure 8.3: Genesis characters and events

Genesis chapters	Events
1. 1–6	Adam and Eve
2. 7–11	The Great Flood with Noah and his family
3. 12–25	Abraham and his family's relationships
4. 26–36	Isaac and Jacob/Israel and their family relationships
5. 37–50	Jacob and Joseph with their families.

These individuals lived approximately 4004 BCE (Adam) to Joseph, who died in 1695 BCE. So, Genesis spans about 2,300 years.

In chapters one to four, God creates the physical world, which provides subject matter for physical sciences, such as biology, astronomy, and zoology that would follow millennia later. Then God forms man and woman, which provide subject matter for sociological study, as well. One could argue, at its core, that Genesis is sociological, since each event's theme revolves around people, most notably families (see Figure 8.3).

Adam and Eve resided in the Garden of Eden where God directed them to increase and multiply (Gen 1:24). This directive establishes humankind's first norm (rule).[7] The earth had lots of room for people, so God told them to fill it. The second norm is a prohibition against eating from the tree of knowledge of good and evil. If they did, God would banish them from Paradise. This injunction establishes the first negative sanction. Afterward, God impressed on man that he should leave his parents and join with a wife. Not only did this instruction institute another norm, but it also anticipated marriage and family institutions.

A *social problem* arises early in Genesis. Cain murdered his brother Abel because God accepted Abel's offering over his. Over the next 1,600 years, metaphorically, humans continued to eat off the tree of knowledge of good and evil as they murdered,

---

7. Part IV presents a few sociological concepts. Part V, however, presents a more comprehensive sociological analysis.

fornicated, and engaged in a plethora of deviant acts.[8] The Lord's patience wore thin, and he caused the Great Flood. This event happened 1,656 years after Adam and Eve were created. Luckily, God recognized some humans as worth saving—Noah and his family.

God instructed him to build an ark and take two of every species on it. When flood waters receded, Noah and his family repopulated the earth. Biblical scholars locate Paradise and the Great Flood in Mesopotamia. Interestingly, many flood stories dating before and after Noah's account describe floods in this region.[9] The Tigris and Euphrates rivers flowed north and south throughout this area, and in the past, it is likely the area flooded in a way similar to how the Nile River flooded Egypt. People wrote stories to cope with and to understand this climatic event. Each story influences narratives that follow. These accounts were adapted to the culture and values of the people writing them. The Gilgamesh Epic, an ancient Mesopotamian story, and the Noah's Ark story helped people in their respective societies deal with life's vicissitudes, such as major flooding. These writings provided their readers with a sense of control over environmental concerns that were otherwise incomprehensible.[10]

Exodus

When I was a kid, I remember seeing the movie *The Ten Commandments* starring Charlton Heston, who played Moses. Most of the film's scenes had to do with the Hebrews exiting Egypt and Moses receiving the Ten Commandments on Mt. Sinai. This film taught me this was the sum and substance of Exodus. You might imagine my surprise when I read the Bible book.

---

8. Religiously, these acts are evil. Sociologically, they are deviant. In either case, these acts fall outside group norms.

9. Ancient Code, "Before Noah's Great Flood."

10. Theologically, the sin was humans disconnected from God's will and divine creatures (i.e., perhaps angels) mating with humans. Their actions created chaos, and to remedy the situation, God unleashed a Great Flood. Enns, "Gilgamesh, Atrahasis and the Flood."

Observations on the Torah/Pentateuch

There is virtually nothing in the film about the scores of laws contained within this book. The Exodus writer sprinkles 108 of God's 613 commandments throughout the book. Examples include: serve God (Exod 23:25), the seventh day of every week is God's Sabbath (Exod 16:23; 23:12), and do not make allies with idol-worshipping nations (Exod 34:15). Laws guided the Israelites on how to deal with personal injuries, property rights, and other day-to-day human encounters.

Moreover, forty-five percent of the book's verses describe sanctuary construction with its interior furnishings. Exodus reads like a woodworkers' handbook and furniture designer's manual. For example, God directs Moses to construct a table

> ... of acacia wood, two cubits long and a cubit wide and one-and-a-half cubits high. He overlaid it with pure gold. He made a rim for it. He cast four gold rings for it and put the rings on the corners that were on its four feet . . (Exod 25:23–26)

How could the universe's God, the creator of this magnificent and immense cosmos, give humans such picayune procedures? Why would he set his mind on such mundane minutia? Was it simply that God had a carpenter's sense? Is that why he picked Joseph to be Mary's husband? This book ends with an accounting of the cost of the tabernacle.[11]

Moses and his complex personality are the stars of Exodus. Although Moses demonstrated a hero's character when he rescued a Hebrew from a fight with an Egyptian (Exod 22:12), he was reticent when God asked him to rescue Hebrews from Egyptian servitude. God persuaded Moses to become a Hebrew liberator only after he promised to get Aaron (Moses' brother) to help him. When Moses confronted the pharaoh, Aaron assisted as his spokesperson.

After successfully tackling the pharaoh, Moses led over 600,000 Hebrews out of Egypt and into the desert. They faced

---

11. As discussed above, the value of the tabernacle is estimated at $86.1 million.

dozens of hostile groups, such as the Amorites and Perizzites. Most notably, they confronted their fears and doubts about their journey with a man claiming to communicate with God. When the Hebrews abandoned Moses and worshipped a false god while he was on the mountain, God directed Moses to kill those who deserted him. About 3,000 men, women, and children died that day.

How in the world did Moses get thousands of people to follow him, especially after claiming to speak to God, and killing thousands of people who followed him through an inhospitable environment for such a long time? Moses grew into his roles as a protector and deliverer. After descending from Mt. Sinai where he visited with God, Exodus says that Moses' hair and complexion changed. He was iridescent. What happened to Moses on that mountain? Believers say God entered Moses' body and grace filled him. Non-believers understand Moses as a true believer whose belief was manifested physically with changes in his body—his hair changed colors, and his face radiated. These bodily changes were similar to the glow attributed to people in love. Moses evolved into a *charismatic* leader. He became an irresistible person who people could not, not hear. Moses was successful in the *arts of impression management*. On some level, Moses knew he had to take charge, and he displayed it through his posture.

Leviticus

Although Leviticus contains the fewest chapters (twenty-seven) in the first five books of the Bible, it records the most laws of any book (244 out of 613, or 39.8 percent). Most of these commandments dealt with religious practices, such as conducting offerings, and rules for the Levite priesthood. Leviticus spells out priests' leadership role. They led services and dressed accordingly. Consequently, the book makes much of how to make priests' garments, what material to use (i.e., linen), and how to wear them (Lev 6:11).

Genesis describes the physical origins of Earth and its inhabitants. It recounts the world's ruin by a global flood, and later its resurrection and rebirth through Noah and his family. It ends with its founder (i.e., Abraham) journeying from Mesopotamia to Canaan and Egypt.

Exodus recounts the Israelites' triumphant exit from Egyptian slavery after 430 years. Then, the book documents forty years of wandering in the desert and the Hebrews' time spent on Mt. Sinai, where Moses received the Ten Commandments. Exodus ends with the Hebrew construction of the tabernacle.

In Leviticus, Moses spells out rituals conducted in the tent of the meeting, sanctuary, and tabernacle. The word "Leviticus" is related to the Levites, that is, Levi's descendants. These priests were the only people permitted entry into the sanctuary, and this prohibition created an exclusive "club" of men with enormous power and influence. These holy men were leaders. The Promised Land was a Holy Land to be organized, settled, and led by priests, not politicians. A theocracy was in development, not a nation. It was to be God's country on Earth.

Numbers

The book of Numbers follows Leviticus. It records events in the second year after the Hebrews left Egypt and while they are on Mt. Sinai and then the Jordan River's banks.

Consequently, Numbers accounts for a large portion of the forty years of wandering in the desert.

The book is an accountant's record of potential soldiers and priests. God was preparing for war against Canaanites and others who occupied the land he'd promised to the Hebrews. After conquering this territory, God calculated how many men were available for service to him as priests. The Israelites, under Moses' guidance, were reluctant followers. They doubted God and Moses at various times after leaving Egypt. They feared, for example, their enemies and dreaded the harsh desert living conditions. They yearned for their time in Egypt where they had plenty of food (Num 14:1–2). Joshua and Caleb, who spied for Moses, squelched these grumblings by insisting the Promised Land met the people's genuine longings.

Part IV: Commentary on the First Five Books of the Bible

The book of Numbers served a cleansing purpose. The Hebrews left Egypt with 603,550 men over twenty years old (Exod 38:26), and they were about to enter the Promised Land with 601,730—were only 1,820 men lost during forty years in the desert? No. They lost *everyone* except Joshua and Caleb, who proved themselves to God. A new generation (Num 26) was about to enter a new land. This fresh start mirrors, in the past, the beginnings Noah brought after the Great Flood as well as, in the future, the New Jerusalem (heaven) Jesus would bring..

Deuteronomy

As the Bible's fifth book, Deuteronomy completes the Jewish Torah and the Christian Pentateuch. "Deuteronomy" means "the repetition of the law." Moses was dying and preparing himself for his journey to heaven in this book. Before he left, however, he repeated the laws and events important in his life. Moses implores the Israelites to obey God's laws. To get them to remember them, he repeats them again and again and again.

Deuteronomy's early chapters read like a travelogue and history book. It reports places the Hebrews passed on their way to the Promised Land and identifies groups who occupied these lands. It retells the hardships they endured during forty years of wandering in the wilderness and recounts their conquests, such as cities in the kingdom of Og and Sihon king of Heshbon (Deut 3:1–6).

Knowing he was in the last stages of his life, Moses was aware he had to transition his *authority* and *power* to others.[12] It was he who was the thread connecting God with the people. When this thread was gone, how were the people to hold together? So in Deuteronomy 1:12–18, he tells the heads of Hebrew tribes to carry on after him. Thus, Moses establishes a line of succession that controlled power and facilitates authority within the Hebrew community. He told them not to be afraid because God would

---

12. Power is A's ability to make B do what B does not necessarily want to do. When power is made legitimate by a social unit, such as a community, it is authority. See, Broom and Selznick, *Sociology*, 704.

Observations on the Torah/Pentateuch

protect them if they kept his commandments. Over and over, Moses reiterated that the Hebrews must live according to the laws of God, because he was their source of their strength and provider of the Promised Land.

If the Israelites incorporated God's message into their lives, his words would bless the land they would occupy. Stay faithful to him, and they would remain intact as a people and possessing the land he'd given them. In other words, God was the bedrock upon which land and people would flourish. Deuteronomy 6:3–4; 7, 13–14; 16–17 state:

> O Israel, you should listen and be careful to do it . . . and that you may multiply greatly, just as the Lord, the God of your fathers, has promised you, in a land flowing with milk and honey. Hear, O Israel! The Lord is our God; the Lord is one! You shall teach diligently to your sons . . . you shall fear only the Lord your God . . . you shall not follow other gods . . . you shall not put the Lord your God to the test . . . you should diligently keep the commandments of the Lord.

God promised them land from the time of their ancestors—Abraham, Isaac, and Jacob—and saved them from Egypt. Their Lord destroyed enemies who occupied the Promised Land. The Lord also constructed a clever interdependence among the people, the book, and the land. The book designated people as "chosen." The Bible asserts its God is the only true god, and the chosen would have a land forever if they abided by his commandments. Who among them would not read this book in perpetuity? Each element of this trinity, consequently, are inextricably connected.[13]

---

13. To this day, politically right-wing Jews in Israel want to annex the West Bank to fulfill, in part, the biblically promised Promised Land. How strong and lasting is their belief in the Torah's verses? How powerful is the Bible that its words reach across 3,000 years of time and fall persuasively on Hebrew eyes in the 21st century?

PART V

Sociological Analysis

CHAPTER 9

A Dramaturgical Analysis of the Torah/Pentateuch

Introduction

WHEN ANY SOCIETY IS under sociological analysis, *Structural-Functionalism*, or simply Functionalism, is generally applied.[1] A Functionalist strives to understand how complex social units create and maintain social order. They seek to understand, for instance, in a crowded stadium of exiting Super Bowl fans, how these people evade bumping into each other. The relative order among them materializes. How is it accomplished?

A Functionalist imagines society as a complex system that seeks equilibrium among its parts. Its parts are institutions. In the present-day United States, when the economy goes awry and people become unemployed, college enrollment increases. That is, when one institution—the economy—goes down, another institution—education—goes up. The net result is a society brought back into harmony or balance, like a see-saw. This analysis represents functional thinking.

Another element in sustaining societal equilibrium is consensus on values. In other words, according to functionalists,

---

1. See Macionis, *Society*.

Part V: Sociological Analysis

when a society maintains harmony, it is because its members agree on their values. So, when societal members value patriotism, recruiting volunteers to serve in the armed forces is not difficult.

Studying the first five books of the Bible from a Functionalist Perspective, it can be surmised that God was a structural-functionalist because most of what God did with the Israelites was to give them rules for living together. Through these rules (613 of them), God defines bad from good behavior, and not only in the religious realm, but also in societal living. He tells people how to deal with neighbors, how judges should properly behave, whom to marry, and how to treat slaves, among other aspects of communal religious and social life. God's rules created order among them. These rules showed Hebrews how to interact with one another within marital, familial, economic, judicial, and religious institutions.

Although functionalism is an apt school for studying Israelite society, a more understandable approach may be dramaturgy. Let's set the stage (no pun intended) for this sociological approach using a theatrical metaphor. Erving Goffman[2] introduced the Dramaturgical Model as a way of understanding human interaction. This model borrowed William Shakespeare's phrase, "All the world's a stage, and all the men and women merely players . . . ."[3] Goffman imagined people as performers in a societal play. When he said *"performer,"* he did not mean people "played at" behavior in society as though they were a bunch of phonies (although some were). He used the term in a descriptive, not prescriptive, sense. He wanted observers to imagine society (i.e., social living) as a play where actors and actresses acted, and they were an audience watching.

To understand how the Dramaturgical Approach applies to the first five books of the Bible, some of its concepts follow.[4]

Rather than call people who live in society "societal members," Goffman calls them *actors* or *actresses*, depending upon

2. Goffman, *Presentation of Self*.
3. Shakespeare, *As You Like It*.
4. Rather than stating the cumbersome Torah/Pentateuch or "first five books of the Bible," I will use simply Torah in this section.

A Dramaturgical Analysis of the Torah/Pentateuch

their sex. The a*udience* were others, that is, people watching a performance.[5] A *script* constituted lines actors and actresses spoke while performing (A traditional sociologist might call script culture). Performers received *boos* (negative sanctions) and *applause* (positive sanctions) depending on a performance's success. A *scene* was a social situation. Actors and actresses performed on the f*ront stage*, while before a presentation, the cast gathered *backstage*. *Masks* were facial expressions, gestures, hand movements, and the like in service of a performance. *Props* (material components of culture) were objects performers used in scenes to assist them in their presentation.

Let's take a scene and apply some dramaturgical concepts. Imagine we are in a bedroom with a husband and wife. The husband says to his wife, "Honey, let's make love." She replies, "I'd love to." No doubt, each of them smiles as they hop into bed. In this scene, the husband is an actor and the wife, an actress. The bed is a prop. Their smile is a mask suggesting they said something appealing and right. Also, their smile was a form of positive sanction or (applause). They acknowledged what each said was right for the situation.

Markings on the floor of the front stage designate where actors and actresses stand. When performers stand on these marks, they hold a specific position or status. Attached to these statuses are expected behaviors or roles. For instance, lifeguards working at a neighborhood pool may wear skimpy bathing suits. However, if they dress this way while attending a church service, they are likely to receive negative sanctions. So the lifeguard status holds different *role expectations* than church-goer status.

Dramaturgical Analysis

The five "acts," under this analysis concept, in the Torah are Genesis, Exodus, Leviticus, Numbers, and Deuteronomy. The curtain went up in Genesis to an empty, dark front stage. The storyteller

---

5. In a real sense, you, the reader, are a member of the audience. You are observing (reading) biblical scenes in this book.

Part V: Sociological Analysis

announced that God created the heavens and the earth, and all within them.[6] In other words, God created scenery for scenes in subsequent acts. Not long after the play began, its first performers stepped on stage—Adam, and shortly afterward, Eve. When they acted on the front stage, sociologists had subject matter to study because they were humans and had interactions.

As the stage light brightened on Adam and Eve, it drew in the audience's attention.[7] The scene was the Garden of Eden. Paradise was pristine. The main props were a serpent and a tree (of knowledge of good and evil). The play's star (i.e., God) told the actor and actress not to eat fruit from this tree or die. With this directive, God established the story's first norm (rule) for performers to obey. In a sense, God created a Diagram of Social Situations. (See chapter two.) His directive established the first vertical lines shown in Figure 9.1.

Figure 9.1: Diagram of Social Situations applied to the Garden of Eden

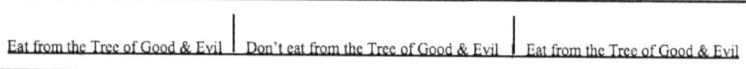

God asserted the behavior that was the norm (i.e., don't eat from the tree). Human action outside of this norm was inappropriate, wrong, or abnormal. As mentioned, initial norms did *not* come from humans. They originated with an otherworldly God. In this sense, sociologist Peter L. Berger argued religion was alienating. How? Rather than recognize fellow humans as creators of their society, religion places its origin in a supra-, non-human, or God-world. Therefore breaking norms makes one not only deviant but also evil. What a powerful way to sustain social compliance, and, with it, social order.[8] Moreover, imaging society's creation as God-given rather than human-made renders power in an otherworldly deity, moving it away from its human origin.

---

6. Tradition holds Moses as the author of these books/acts.
7. Today, the audience is 39 million people who have bought the Bible.
8. Berger, *Sacred Canopy*.

A Dramaturgical Analysis of the Torah/Pentateuch

In act two (i.e., Exodus), God presented his first collection of norms. This established rules for the Hebrews as a group and statutes for the sons of Israel as individuals. Before the people could initiate these directives, though, God's authenticity had to be established for these Hebrews to "buy into" what he said. Religious commandments concentrated on determining God as authentically true and worthy of following, worshipping, and celebrating. He said:

> I am the Lord thy God, who brought you out of the land of Egypt, out of the house of slavery. You shall have no other gods before Me. You shall not make for yourself an idol or any likeness . . You shall not worship them or serve them . . . . (Exod 20:2–5).

After God established himself as the true God, the authentic star of the play, he detailed worshipping procedures for himself.[9] He created a religious ceremony (Passover) and provided specifics on:

1. How and when to conduct this ceremony—staging techniques and timing.
2. Who could and could not participate in it—legitimate cast members.
3. What the purpose was—the play's theme.
4. What appropriate gifts for God were—props.
5. Who and how presiders of this ceremony were to dress—props and masks.
6. What items (e.g., oil and incense) were to be used during this ceremony—props.

Passover commemorated the moment God "passed over" Hebrew homes in Egypt as he killed every other firstborn human and animal. This ceremony functioned as a *bonding vehicle*

---

9. Consider that there was no God in heaven who claimed to be the true God, but rather the author telling this story (i.e., Moses) projected this assertion upon this God.

Part V: Sociological Analysis

for Hebrews through Passover rituals, such as eating and praying together. These practices moved maunders into a group. A person within this group prayed over and over again. As a mnemonic device, prayer socialized a roaming slave in a desert into a Hebrew who belonged to a group chosen by God. A play's cast was forming.

The second set of Exodus commandments concentrated on human relations. God gave directives for treating parents, neighbors, and slaves. Biblical scholars think these ordinances curtailed violence toward others. They showed how people who lived in an agrarian society should treat domesticated animals, such as oxen and donkeys. They guided people in business relations, such as making loans. These ordinances recognized two foundational principles of human relationships: trust and justice. The rules warned about what would undermine fundamental trust among them.

> You shall not hear a false report; do not join your hand with a wicked man to be a malicious witness ... nor shall you testify in a dispute to turn aside after a multitude to pervert justice (Exod 23:1–2).
>
> Keep from a false charge, and do not kill the innocent or the righteous, for I will not acquit the guilty. You shall not take a bribe, for a bribe blinds the clear-sighted and subverts the cause of the just (Exod 23:7–8).

Essentially, Exodus's plot deepened the narrative that told the story of a loose assemblage of wanderers with developing rules that pulled them together into a cohesive working group.

Exodus 21 concentrated on the treatment of slaves. Although it might be tempting to condemn the Bible for acknowledging slavery, we do not wish to commit the *Dillingham Flaw*. That is, we do not aim to apply today's standards to judge yesterday's practices.[10] Exodus 21:2–4, 7–8, and 10 showed how masters should treat their slaves.

> If you buy a Hebrew slave, he shall serve for six years; but on the seventh, he shall go out as a free man without payment ... if he is the husband of a wife, then his

---

10. Parillo, *Strangers to these Shores*.

wife shall go out with him. If his master gives him a wife, and she bears him sons or daughters, the wife and her children shall belong to her master . . If a man sells his daughter as a female slave, *she is not to go free as the male slaves do*. If she is displeasing in the eyes of her master who designated her for himself, then he shall let her be redeemed. If he takes to himself another woman, *he may not reduce her food, her clothing, or her conjugal rights* [Italics added].

These directives pertained only to Hebrew slaves. They were not in servitude for life as slaves in other groups at that time. Masters freed their Hebrew slaves after six years of service. A slave given a wife by his master was free, but not his wife and their children. After all, they were a master's property. In another situation, if a master sold his daughter into slavery, the new master wedded her, and she received provisions for her protection, according to biblical scholars. The unequal treatment of men and women is evident within the institution of slavery. Although owners could free male slaves, they did not free female slaves. On the other hand, displeased owners of female slaves could not mistreat their female slaves as noted by italics in the above quoted material.

This narrative differentiated pagan slave practices from Hebrew practices. In the Hebrew rendition of the slave story, the Israelites introduced a more humane approach, but they still retained the plotline of slavery.

Exodus 21–23 dealt with other forms of human dealings, such as personal injury and property rights. Exodus 21 handled involuntary manslaughter and murder. If a man did not mean to kill another, but he died, the culprit was set free. If a man knowingly killed another, the perpetrator died. If a master hit his slave who did *not* die, there was no punishment. Why? The slave was his property!

The abovementioned rights developed into Hebrew norms that provided laws and social order. A social structure was forming and its origin was otherworldly.

Part V: Sociological Analysis

The most recognizable ordinances in Exodus are the Ten Commandments (Exod 20:3–17):

1. You shall have no other gods before me.
2. You shall not make for yourself an idol or any other likeness.
3. You shall not take the name of the Lord your God in vain.
4. Remember the Sabbath day.
5. Honor your father and your mother.
6. You shall not murder.
7. You shall not commit adultery.
8. You shall not steal.
9. You shall not bear false witness against your neighbor.
10. You shall not covet your neighbor's house, wife, male servant, female servant, ox, donkey, or anything that belongs to your neighbor.

Commandments number one through four told Hebrews to respect and worship God. The remaining six mandates guided them in human relationships, first with parents by honoring them and all other associations. Commandments six and eight commended Hebrews to be faithful to life and property. Commandment seven protected the institution of marriage, while ten protected marriage and property. Thus, the stability of marital and familial units—bedrocks of society—were reinforced in these commandments. Also, commandment nine informed Hebrews to keep true to their word.

These commandments, except four and five, informed Hebrews what they should *not* do. Accordingly, eight commandments explained behaviors falling outside of normative borders on the diagram, and these commandments deemed these behaviors inappropriate, psychologically abnormal, or morally wrong. Exodus 21–23 developed the Exodus plotline by presenting God's norms

A Dramaturgical Analysis of the Torah/Pentateuch

to the Hebrews and urging them to adhere. The Diagram of Social Situations lists the Ten Commandments in Figure 9.2.[11]

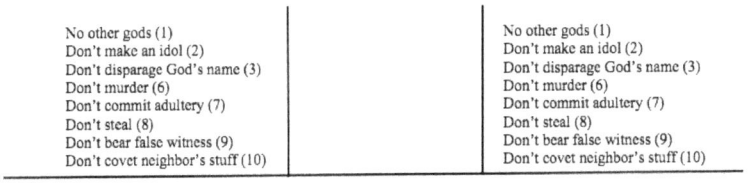

Figure 9.2: Ten Commandments incorporated into the Diagram of Social Situations

No other gods (1)	No other gods (1)
Don't make an idol (2)	Don't make an idol (2)
Don't disparage God's name (3)	Don't disparage God's name (3)
Don't murder (6)	Don't murder (6)
Don't commit adultery (7)	Don't commit adultery (7)
Don't steal (8)	Don't steal (8)
Don't bear false witness (9)	Don't bear false witness (9)
Don't covet neighbor's stuff (10)	Don't covet neighbor's stuff (10)

Let us recap the biblical story to this point. In the beginning, God created Adam and Eve. They sinned and God banished them from Eden. Later they had children. About 1,000 years passed when God told Noah he would flood the earth. Noah built an Ark and he took two of every living creature on board. The Flood ended after forty days and forty nights. The Ark landed on a mountain top in present-day Turkey. Later, God sacked Sodom and Gomorrah.

Nearly 400 years afterward, Abraham moved the Hebrews out of Mesopotamia toward land promised to them by God. Isaac and later Jacob assumed leadership of the people after Abraham died. They led wandering masses of Israelites toward the Promised Land.

Less than one hundred years passed when Joseph's brothers sold him into Egyptian slavery, where he lived and prospered.[12] Then, Joseph returned to his homeland to bring the entire Hebrew people to Egypt. When they arrived, a new pharaoh enslaved the Israelites. They remained slaves for 430 years.

An Egyptian princess found a Hebrew baby, Moses, in a basket floating down the Nile and raised him as a royal. Once Moses saw a Hebrew beaten by an Egyptian soldier. He defended the Hebrew by taking the Egyptian's life. Fearing capture, Moses fled Egypt.

God summoned Moses back to Egypt to lead his people out of slavery. Moses, assisted by his brother Aaron, led hundreds

---

11. The number in parentheses identifies the specific commandment.
12. A descendant of Abraham, Isaac, and Jacob/Israel.

of thousands of Israelites through a parted Red Sea to Mt. Sinai. There God appeared to Moses in a burning bush and gave him Ten Commandments and other ordinances. Later, Moses moved the Israelites to the border of the Promised Land. He died, and God buried him.

This five-act play, at its root, tells a story of disorganized people running away from slavery. They survived for forty years in a hostile desert environment on their way to a land of milk and honey. God above, it was said, presented hundreds of rules to secure these peoples' physical survival and later to have them honor him as their Lord.

Artifacts, as material components of culture, assisted in telling this holy story. They set scenes in the play. One prop used was the Ark of the Covenant that held the Ten Commandments, which was held within another prop, the tent of meeting. This tent had other material items of culture, such as a bronze altar, linen curtains, and a golden lampstand. Priests paid great attention to stitching together garments, including robes, tunics, and turbans, for priests who entered the tent. These props were made of wool, linen, or leather (Lev 13:47–48) and had breast pieces with Urim and Thummim embedded in them (Lev 8:8). These elements were a source of revelation, thus rendering priests conduits between God and his people. These elements gave priests enormous power within the Hebrew community because only they communicated directly with the Almighty. These garments served as symbols of their power within their community.

The Bible records cultural differences in its first five acts. Genesis 43 recounted that Egyptians were unwilling to sit and eat bread with Hebrews because they considered them loathsome. In Genesis 34, however, Hamor wanted Jacob to have his sons and daughters intermarry so they all could openly trade and acquire some property. Consequently, Hamor sought a *multi-cultural* and globalist stance between his people and Hebrews. The scene, however, did not end well. Jacob's sons sacked Hamor's city in retribution for their sister, who was raped by Hamor's son.

A Dramaturgical Analysis of the Torah/Pentateuch

An intimate marriage and family issue provided a scene in Leviticus, revolving around the issue of who could have sex with whom. Twelve commandments in Leviticus addressed sexual relations with relatives. Why were they presented? Some contend the incest taboo is a *cultural universal*, a social item found in every culture. Several scholars argue prohibitions against sex with blood relatives protected families from producing biologically defective members. Others claim these bans served a social function.

Frequently bonds of marriage and family life are fragile, especially over long periods of time living together. Family members see one another in their best and worst times, seven days a week, for years. What if people introduced courting into this delicate social unit? If a son wooed his mother, or a daughter dated her dad, imagine how jealous family members could get. Visualize how these conditions could weaken a family unit already prone to instability.

How do societal members obtain their group's script that defines reality? They get it from those who have it—their socializing agents. Initially, the script originated with God in heaven. He socialized Adam and Eve into seeing their actions as right or wrong. As the story went on, God functioned like a chorus in Greek plays. Like this Greek chorus, God was the play's director, or, as a sociologist would say, a socializing agent; he showed people how to behave. Continuing this analogy, as Greek plays developed over time, actors on the front stage took over more action independent of the chorus. Similarly, this describes the Bible's story. How? (Figure 9.3 shows God's mind with a Diagram of Social Situations embedded in it).

Part V: Sociological Analysis

Figure 9.3: God as socializing agent

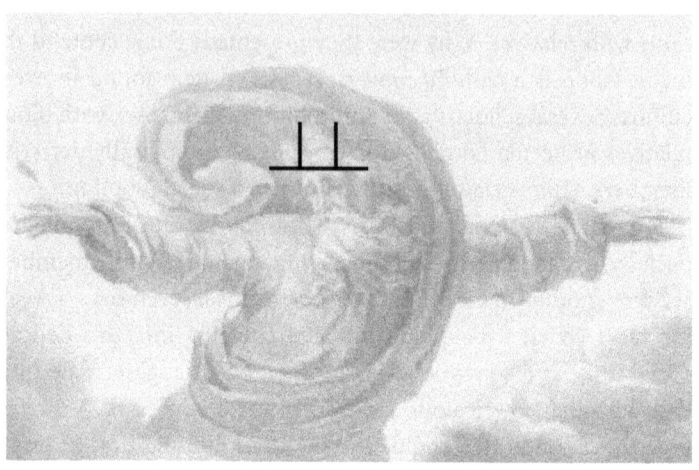

Source: Library of Congress, public domain. Modifications added.

God, in heaven, told Adam and Eve how to behave. Later, they acted independently of the Lord. Said differently, God, as a socializing agent, had a diagram in his head (See Figure 9.3). He presented this diagram to Adam and Eve (i.e., socializees). Once people *internalized* a diagram (and other ones), it controlled them. When they acted by the diagram, Adam and Eve understood they behaved appropriately, normally, or correctly. Adam and Eve socialized new people, most notably Cain and Abel, and later Seth. Socializing agents employed positive (i.e., rewards) and negative (i.e., punishments) sanctions to encourage and discourage socializees' actions, in order to be consistent with their group's diagrams. So, after Cain killed Abel, God punished Cain, the deviant, by ruining his land for growing crops (Gen 4:12).

Although humans took over some socializing agent functions at this stage of human development, God still gave the Israelites commandments through Moses. The passage of control of human behavior, according to the story, did not rest totally with humans.

A Dramaturgical Analysis of the Torah/Pentateuch

In Genesis 3, however, Adam was as a socializing agent when he named Eve. Through their interaction, Eve acquired an identity. This socialization process persisted throughout Genesis. In Genesis 17, God changed Abram's name to Abraham and Sarai's name to Sarah. In Genesis 35, God changed Jacob's name to Israel. On each occasion, as socializees followed the directions of socializing agents, their identities changed in recognition of their closeness with the deity. Undoubtedly, changing their status in this fashion made these individuals "special" among their peers. It was as if these performers received special billing in a play's program.

Consequently, this action gave these people power within their group. The ultimate identity claim happened in Genesis 5 when God said he made man in his image.

We see change on multiple levels. Personal status with the deity changed; individuals' names changed; and the group's identity was altered from slaves to a chosen people. Being recognized by God made them chosen; their name change realized this transformation, and they were no longer vagabonds but children of a true God.

Audience members witness a universal story told with the same motif throughout the ages with different characters and plots. These stories tell the human saga; that is, while we live our lives, forces threaten us that we have little control over. Hurricanes, earthquakes, and viral pandemics threaten us, and we cannot stop them. This storyline was told in Greek times by the *Odyssey*, while in the Middle Ages, it was *Beowulf*, and in modern times Harry Potter. Some heroes find the source of their strength within themselves, while others find it outside of them. In this latter type, one place to find resolve was in God, as told in biblical stories.

Labeling is another act of socialization, as in Genesis 17, when God made a covenant with Abram. God directed him to circumcise males in his group as a mark of their allegiance to the Lord. The Israelites ritualized these actions in the centuries that followed. Its importance was overwhelming. To be so marked meant one belonged to a group God chose as his own. Power—instilled in them—justified them doing anything, as long as it was in the name

Part V: Sociological Analysis

of the Lord. So, when the Israelites arrived at the Promised Land, they could remove its inhabitants by force because God directed them to do so. Consequently, this was not ethnic cleansing; it was a holy action required by God.

In Leviticus 11, God socialized Moses into dietary laws. He showed Moses which species of animal were edible from those that were not. Fish *with* fins and scales were permissible, while those without were not (see Figure 9.4 below).

Figure 9.4 God's diagram for humans eating fish

Fish *without* fins & scales	Fish *with* fins & scales	Fish *without* fins & scales

The Bible prohibited eating bats, but locusts were acceptable (see Figure 9.5 below).

Figure 9.5 God's diagram for humans eating locusts

Bats	Locusts	Bats

Motifs in the Torah performances were: God created the world, man fell, God saved him, Hebrews moved from Mesopotamia toward Canaan, they moved to Egypt, and returned to the Promised Land's threshold.

By Deuteronomy's time, the biblical story showed people maturing in religion and social living. Their faith formed a priesthood of socializing agents who taught laymen, women, and children (socializees). Accordingly, the scene on stage was Hebrew priests reading and studying laws in preparation for preaching and publishing them. They were training themselves to be socializing agents, and they prepared socializees for participation within Hebrew society. (Deut 6:7) Priests from the religious sphere socialized others in and for the societal realm. Religion and social life, subsequently, were intricately connected.

When socializees internalized God's rules, they behaved automatically by them. It was as if socializees moved on stage without direction because they had internalized lines from their script.

A Dramaturgical Analysis of the Torah/Pentateuch

Consequently, it was not necessary to visibly tell them what to do. They acted in appropriate ways automatically. They no longer needed direction.

Essentially, what we saw on stage happened in Hebrew society. As actors and actresses internalize lines from their script, they act automatically by its content. They no longer need direction, and order permeates the stage. In a like manner, as the Hebrews internalized socialization from their socializing agents (i.e., priests), they acted automatically. Since most of them did so, social order permeated their society. Those who deviated from Hebrew law behaved inappropriately, abnormally, or wrongly.

Socialization was not a "once-and-done" proposition. Every week, it continued at religious services where priests taught commandments and every seven years when Hebrews gathered to read the Law. (Deut 31:10–13) As Moses proselytized Hebrews into this religious dogma (Deut 31:19), no doubt they imagined themselves to be devout people. They were not merely citizens in a civil society; they were people of God. They were forming and living in a theocracy.

God communicated commandments about the forbidden, such as worshipping false gods (Deut 12:2–4), and nations that supported them had to be destroyed (Deut 20:17). They were forbidden to learn (Deut 12:3) or teach (Deut 13:12–14) false gods, so they could not give into, spare, or protect anyone who taught about false gods (Deut 13:8). God was moving the Hebrews away from non-Hebrews with these commandments.

Consequently, he was proclaiming that the beliefs and practices of "others" fell outside the Hebrew diagram. This action pulled Hebrews together. As they looked toward one another, they saw themselves as a group. In other words, a Hebrew identity was forming. Part of this identity was that they were a chosen people as God selected them. As they realized this aspect of their "selves," some may have felt superior to others. These individuals were forming an *ethnocentric* persona.[13]

---

13. Ethnocentrism is the belief one's way of life is superior to another's.

Part V: Sociological Analysis

Another element of this religious formation was God's role. The Lord told Hebrews they could not test him by doubting or rebelling against him. This commandment ensured God was a central and sole focus. What was shaping up was a show with a lone star on stage that drew everyone's attention—God, the one true Lord. Thus, society was forming based on a new religion that had the one true God. It was as if a braid composed of three interwoven strands was under development:

1. The Israelites were forming as a group.
2. A society was residing in the Promised Land.
3. The people were abiding by commandments coming from the one, true God.

Essentially, this was the Torah's trinity.

Rituals and ceremonies reinforced the development of and adherence to religious laws. Props, such as temples, were constructed to house God. Priests performed services at God's sanctuary (prop) at appointed times (Deut 18:6–8). Ceremonies, in the form of feasts, were held in God's place (Deut 12:5–7; 14). Socialization continued as socializing agents told the faithful to appear before God and rejoice at feasts (Deut 16:14). They brought tithes and offerings (Deut 12:5–6) to these ceremonies. Practicing these rites reinforced people's belief in the religion they observed, and their gathering together strengthened their bond with one another.

The infusion of God's laws through Moses and into the Hebrew people led believers to listen to and obey God's anointed ones: priests and elders (Deut 18:15–19; 17:8–13). Authority was vested in them. As judges of the law, they had power (Deut 13:14). Since they interpreted the law, guilt was determined by how they judged a person's actions (Deut 19:19). Thus, a society based on a new religion was forming. The Israelites were developing a Diagram of Social Situations to structure their communal life, socially and religiously.

After establishing the Hebrew religion and its leaders as a central part of Israelite life, community members solidified other aspects of public living. The congregation cared for the poor (Deut 15:8; 11); freed slaves (Deut 15:12-14; 18); and established monetary arrangements. For example, the Israelites charged foreigners interest on loans (Deut 23:21); those suffering body damages were compensated (Deut 25:11-12); and workers received pay on time (Deut 24:15).

Just as scaffolding can hold up the scenery in a play, institutions provide a platform for societies. When a society needs to satisfy its members' physical needs, it creates rules for distributing goods and services. In other words, it designs an economic institution. When a society needs new members to replace its old ones, it needs a way to indoctrinate these new members. Norms (rules) guide these activities, which lead to marriage and family institutions.

The creation scene in Genesis showed how God populated the earth through Adam and Eve and their descendants. The Bible mentioned marriage and family often, as it cited polygamous, and most notably, *polygynous* marriage forms.[14] In Genesis 4:19, Methuselah's son, Lamech, had two wives (Adah and Zillah). Later, in Genesis 16:3, Abraham took Sarah and Hagar as his wives, and then he took another wife (Keturah) (Gen 25:1). Today Western societies consider polygamous marriages deviant, but in biblical times they were commonplace. Why? Not many people populated the planet in its beginning. "To increase and multiply," as the Deity directed, had its best chance if the marital arrangement permitted more women producing children (polygamy) than fewer women (monogamy).

Genesis 29 and 38 revealed two familial norms: birth order and lineage. First, although Jacob wanted to marry Rachel, he married Leah. Since Rachel was the second daughter, she had to wait until her older sister married. Second, Er was married to Tamar, but God killed Er for being evil. His father (Judah) ordered Er's brother (Onan) to marry Tamar. He refused because their offspring would not carry his name, so he spilled his seed on the ground. Both situations happened because of customs in their culture.

---

14. Polygyny is a marriage form which includes one man with multiple women.

Part V: Sociological Analysis

The scene changed in Leviticus. After it established rules for marriage and family life, our biblical play presented its concern about the sacred. Approximately fifty-eight percent of the commandments in Leviticus focused on religious behavior. Together, these norms formed the Hebrew religion as an institution.

Twelve Leviticus commandments launched monotheistic religion. These ensured Hebrews worshipped the one God while it deemed other gods "false." God's laws prohibited Israelites from worshipping spiritualists, such as mediums and family spirits (Lev 19:31). Other widespread religious practices were forbidden, too, such as astrology and fortune-telling (Lev 19:27). Leviticus's practices brought a new religious concept: a unitary God. Once many gods populated heaven, and now only one did.

Other religious mandates focused on sacrifices, feasts, the Sabbath, and care of the sanctuary. Together, these directives coalesced into a set of norms forming a religious institution. This new religion introduced *rituals* and *ceremonies*. A ritual is a group of actions performed for symbolic value. A ceremony is done on certain occasions to bring people together, often in celebration.[15] If a person thoughtlessly swears, for example, he engages in a guilt offering. In this ritual, the sinner brings an offering to a priest, who offers it up to God on his behalf (Lev 5:4–6).

Religions create a guardian class who administer, represent, and protect the institution. Hebrews had a priestly class overseeing it. Who were they? Moses said God declared Aaron and his sons priests (i.e., Levites) (Lev 21:1).

This priestly group created rules to establish purity within this religious group, so priests could not marry harlots or anyone failing to denounce false gods (Lev 21:6–8, 21:7, 21:14). Thus, these rules ensured the purity of the body and religion. Moreover, a priestly class is typically not egalitarian; some have higher status, as evident in the new Hebrew religion. Twelve commandments established a priestly stratification, since there were "high" priests mentioned, suggesting lower ones were also serving (Lev 21:11).

---

15. Aron. "Difference Between Rituals and Ceremonies."

A Dramaturgical Analysis of the Torah/Pentateuch

Other commandments focused on social matters. Decrees instructed the sons of Israel in dietary law, how judges must behave, how to give loans, how to conduct business, and how to supervise slaves. Thirteen commandments regulated Hebrew economic relations. God expected people not to oppress, take advantage of, or defraud others (Lev 19:11, 19:13, 25:14, 25:17). He prohibited withholding a hired man's wages beyond its expected time (Lev 19:13). He prohibited Hebrews from charging interest on loans to their countrymen. God did not prohibit slavery, but he expected fair treatment of the enslaved (Lev 25:43).

Leviticus and Deuteronomy possessed commandments that shaped the judiciary and legal institutions. In Leviticus 19, commandments guided the Hebrews in how to judge one another. God's laws forbade Hebrews from failing to report a sin (i.e., breaking God's law) or not testifying in an investigation. Examples of judges' behavior were that they had to be just, could not render a judgment based on their opinion, and not slander anyone. God was demanding judges to be fair, unbiased, and just. Accomplishing these standards meant a society would operate in an orderly manner.

The Lord extended his directives on the judicial system in Deuteronomy. A judge had to know the law (Deut 1:13), not accept false testimony (Deut 19:16–17), and not punish an innocent crime victim (Deut 22:26). Defendants had protections. Judges could not adjudicate suspects based on: 1. Their parent or children's actions. (Deut 24:16); or 2. The testimony of a single witness or circumstantial evidence (Deut 19:15). If a judge announced a sentence, he carried it out to its fullest (Deut. 17:11–12), but not more than required by law (Deut 25:2–3).

Commandments addressed the conduct of a head of state, specifically he should not:

1. Be a stranger (Deut 17:15).

2. Be ruled by his wives.(Deut 17:17).

3. Put his trust in military power (Deut 17:16).

4. Be governed by a lust for wealth (Deut 17:17).

Part V: Sociological Analysis

Finally, in plays, actors and actresses deal with tragedy or problems. On the one hand, difficulties demonstrate imperfections in these characters or their situations, while on the other, disasters make characters stronger.

Genesis was replete with social problems. Unacceptable (by their standards) group and personal behavior ran rampant. For instance, the biblical narrative describing Paradise included social problems. The most prominent among them, mentioned, at least eight times, was murder. Cain murdered his brother Abel because God favored Abel's offering over his own (Gen 4:8). Lamech, Methushael's son, killed a man for wounding him and a boy for striking him (Gen 4:23). God told Abraham to sacrifice his son, Isaac, but the Lord withdrew his directive (Gen 22:2). Simeon and Levi (Dinah's brothers) murdered every male in Hamor's city because Hamor raped Dinah (Gen 34:25). Joseph's brothers plotted to kill him but decided to sell him into Egyptian slavery. God killed Er, Judah's firstborn, because he judged him evil (Gen 38:7). Later, Moses killed an Egyptian for beating a Hebrew (Ex 2:12).

In many contemporary societies, homosexuality and masturbation are not social problems. Sexual intercourse, however, was the basis for many social problems in the Bible. Lot hid men in his house to protect them from the homosexual urges of townsmen, and Onan spilled his seed on the ground rather than impregnate his deceased brother's wife.

Although today slavery is abhorrent, it was not in biblical times. God invoked commandments against mistreating Hebrew slaves, but he did not condemn this institution. Biblical scholars argue that Hebrew law provided for the humane treatment to slaves in comparison to other groups at that time. For instance, Hebrew slaves had a term of "service" that lasted six years. Slavery did not last a lifetime as in other contemporaneous groups.

Other social problems occurred among the Hebrews wandering in the desert, including thievery and bribery. A thief appeared before a judge for punishment (Exod 22:8). Taking bribes could subvert a person's judgment, and this deviant behavior could weaken justice among his group (Exod 23:8).

A Dramaturgical Analysis of the Torah/Pentateuch

Plays are mediums for portraying life. As we watch actors and actresses perform on a stage, we draw lessons from their actions. Imagining the first five biblical books as acts in a play, what instructions do readers receive?

One can argue we have viewed an allegorical representation. That is, the story reveals a hidden moral and political meaning. Remember, the play's author and the central character is Moses. Portrayed as a shy and quiet man, he felt incapable of leadership. Additionally, the Israelites—a cast of thousands—were a vagabond collection of weary slaves just freed from captivity. So, on individual and group levels, the audience sees some "losers," while others become the chosen people, with one rising to become the leader. On the face of it, it is a story about the rise of the Hebrew nation—its people and land blessed by God. On another level, we have a story about a feeble individual and disheveled group. At its root, the Torah presents a *constructed reality* whose details follow.

The fourth book of the Bible, Numbers, chronicled the time when the Israelites moved from the desert they'd inhabited for almost forty years to arriving at the land promised to them by God (but not occupying the land). Remember the scene. First, Moses was a reluctant leader. He was shy and disinclined to approach the pharaoh to ask him anything, let alone to release the Israelites from bondage. He relied on his brother, Aaron, to speak for him (Exod 3–4). Second, he knew Canaanites occupied the Promised Land and lived in fortified cities. His people, on the other hand, were loosely bonded, nomadic, and unarmed. Moses, however, became a successful leader. How?

A two-part process explains it. First, Moses told the Israelites, over and over, that God spoke to him. As he asserted this claim, he came to believe it. In other words, his assertion became a *self-fulfilling prophecy*. He acted in ways he came to think he could.

Consequently, he took more significant risks that panned out, such as heading out into an extremely arid desert. Yet they survived for forty years.

As Moses accomplished more and more feats, he was filled with confidence and his belief welled up and sprung out. His demeanor changed. Assurance and conviction filled his face. It was as if he wore a mask of charisma that inspired others. (Believers may call this grace.)

Second, he claimed the source of his legitimacy arose not from himself but from God. Moses was a deferential and timid man. God used him as his instrument of delivery. Moses asserted that God saved the Israelites from extinction in the desert, not himself. As Moses framed the situation: someone who was against him was really opposing God, not Moses, the individual. The reality that Moses constructed created believers and non-believers—not in Moses, but in God. These actions brought power to Moses and to the people who believed his assertions. On another level, this belief system socially controlled believers. Accordingly, they became subservient to their leader, and this established social order among them.

Within this constructed reality, the Israelites were moving toward land promised to them by God. Canaanites lived there, so these occupiers had to be forcefully removed. Within this constructed reality, Canaanites became the "enemy." Midianites, also, were non-believers that inhabited nearby territory. They, too, had to be eradicated for the same reason. Not surprisingly, the first chapter of Numbers described a census of Israelite warriors, an assessment of their military power. Chapter two told how to arrange the Hebrew army in their encampment; they were preparing for war.

The Israelites believed in commandments that brought social order; they labeled those who went against these ordinances deviants, such as lepers and manslayers. Lepers were unclean. The Lord permitted only clean people in his presence. Thus, lepers became symbols of non-believers. They were unclean and, consequently, reprehensible. They needed to be cast out (or redeemed). However, on a secular level, this belief minimized disease among the Israelites, which allowed their population to grow. The Hebrews executed manslayers or murderers. When tempers flared among people living in close proximity, what this law prohibited was a check on them from killing one another. This safeguard enhanced the longevity of the group.

A Dramaturgical Analysis of the Torah/Pentateuch

From Abraham's time in Genesis to the day Moses died in Deuteronomy, interactions between the Israelites and their God transformed these people. They started as a loose collection of individuals when they left Egypt, wandering in the desert. Then God gave them hundreds of laws to govern their behavior. These norms transformed them into a cohesive group with an identity as God's chosen people. At this point, they became a nation.

Believers understand the Bible as the word of God. Sociologists neither approve nor disapprove of this belief. They take an *un*respectable (not *dis*respectful) view of this matter.[16] Sociologists look at religious behavior as if they were *in* this world but not *of* it, taking a dispassionate view of religious performance. When they do, they see how human interaction creates the social world humans inhabit. Believers understand that the Israelites destroyed Midianites because God directed them (Num 31). Sociologists observe how the Israelites interacted with one another to establish a reason for engaging and killing the Midianites as "enemies."

On a societal plane, descendants of the chosen (Israelites) currently fight over the land they believe God granted them. Palestinians lay claim to this same territory. How will today's Middle Eastern conflict between Israelites and Palestinians be resolved? Arabs have lived there for centuries, while Israelites believe God gave them this land epochs ago.

Finally, although the Torah/Pentateuch presented Moses' and the Israelites' transformation from vulnerable to invincible, these books inform their readers that they, too, may make this conversion. The biblical story invests the power of this change in a suprabeing that was not of this world (i.e., God). Although sociology does not take a stand on what one *should* believe in, readers of the sociological perspective may wonder if these words mean there is a power within them and not outside in an otherworldly God. Sociology does *not* advance such a position. Nonetheless, this viewpoint may move one to this outlook after applying a sociological perspective to biblical phenomena. Why? This position notes that "human" behavior results from "human" action. In this sense,

---

16. See Berger, "Sociology as a Form of Consciousness."

Part V: Sociological Analysis

many believers find sociology a subversive discipline. Where does the source of one's being lay? Is it inside or outside of us? I leave it to readers to decide on this issue.

PART VI

Conclusion

CHAPTER 10

Finale

As FIGURE 10.1 SHOWS, the first five books of the Bible contain a total of 187 chapters and 5,834 verses. While Genesis is the most verbose, Leviticus is the most succinct. Moreover, Genesis records the most individuals while Leviticus logs the most laws.

Figure 10.1: Torah/Pentateuch chapters and verses

Book	No. of Chapters	No. of Verses
Genesis	50	1,515
Exodus	40	1,213
Leviticus	27	859
Numbers	36	1,288
Deuteronomy	<u>34</u>	<u>959</u>
TOTALS:	*187*	*5,834*

We have covered much ground in the first five books of the Bible. We have traveled from the beginning of time to Moses' death in 1407 BCE, totaling nearly 2,600 years. In regards to space, we started in the Garden of Eden in Mesopotamia, went to Egypt,

Part VI: Conclusion

and wound up in the Promised Land of Canaan (present-day Israel). Today, from the mouth of the Persian Gulf in southern Iraq to Israel is approximately 1,040 miles. From Jerusalem, Israel to Cairo is about 200 miles. Collectively, the biblical Israelites walked nearly 1,240 miles, plus 380 miles of wandering in the desert for a total of approximately 1,600 miles. While covering this territory, the Israelites contacted scores of ethnic groups, such as Ammonites, Jebusites, Canaanites, and Egyptians.

This biblical narrative is about God's actions toward the people he chose as his own. The Lord displayed a range of emotions toward them. Among them were love, anger, protection, and obliteration. He made agreements with Hebrew men, such as Abraham, Isaac, and Jacob. These relationships and covenants between God and the Hebrews spanned centuries.

Commandments (613 of them) regulated God's relationship with his chosen people. Moses wrote down these laws into the Torah/Pentateuch; they directed the Israelites in religious and secular practices. These traditions shaped their personal and collective lives. Additionally, these commandments fashioned a unique identity of the Israelites as God's chosen people.

This presentation answered six fundamental questions about the Bible's first five books: who, what, when, where, why, and how (see Figure F.10.2).

Finale

Figure 10.2: Summary of the first five Bible books

	Gen		Exod		Lev		Num		Deut	
	Indivs.	Grps.	Indivs.	Grps.	Indivs.	Grps.	Indivs.	Grps.	Indivs.	Grps.
WHO?	300+	several	93	16	15	2	(Censuses cited too) Israelis warriors = 603,550 Levite priests = 22,300 202	75	41	43
WHAT?	Beginning of everything to Joseph's death in Egypt. Creation, destruction, and reconstruction and covenants		Sons of Israel in Egypt accounted; Moses birth; Moses leads Hebrews out of Egypt and receives the Ten Commandments; to tabernacle & tent of meeting erected		God spoke to Moses about religious rules & rules for priests; to implement them; to all details finished on Mt. Sinai.		Censuses in Sinai Wilderness to commandments/ordinances given on Moab Plains by the Jordan across from Jericho, and readied to enter Promised Land		In 40th year across from Jericho to Moses' death; Moses' swan song	
WHEN?	4004 to 1695 BCE About twenty-five generations from Adam		1525 to 1445 BCE About 355 years from Jacob's time in Egypt to Tabernacle erected, but mostly in 1846-45 BCE		1445 BCE 244 commandments given while on Mt. Sinai, likely in one year		1445 to 1407 BCE Probably 2nd year after leaving Egypt and most of the time during wilderness wanderings		1407 to 1406 BCE In the 40th year of wandering, 1st day of the 11th month to Moses' death	
WHERE?	Garden of Eden—Mesopotamia (southern Iraq) to Mt. Ararat (Turkey) to Canaan (Israel), to Egypt		Egypt to Wilderness and Mt. Sinai		Mt. Sinai		Mt. Sinai to Wilderness of Paran to Wilderness of Zin at Kadesh to Mt. Hor by Red Sea (part of Jordan and Saudi Arabia) to Land of Moab (today-Jordan) by Jordan River opposite Jericho		Across the Jordan River in the Land of Moab to Moab Plains to the top of Mt. Nebo, where Moses died (Jordan)	
WHY?	Described physical & social creation, destruction, and rebirth		God's bargain with the Hebrews: accept Me, you get the Promised Land		God directed the Israelis: how to properly behave, survive the desert, and how to properly worship God		They counted the new generation		Moses' last hurrah: restated God's laws as preparation to enter Promised Land & revisited lessons learned through his life	
HOW?	Moses believed to be Torah/Pentateuch's author; was challenging to read.		Leaving Egypt plus many laws/rules for tabernacle construction		How to: approach God, good social relationships, good hygiene, and acceptable eating practices		God "figured" out the numbers of men fielding an army and serving in the priesthood		Second time stating God's laws, indicating their extreme importance	

NOTE: "Indivs." means individuals while "Grps." means groups.

These books are replete with individuals and groups. Although the Bible records scores of people, overwhelmingly they are males. The Bible is a book about a patriarchy.

These five books chronicle travelers who first departed Mesopotamia in search of the Promised Land, and later they left Egypt after 430 years of slavery. Guided by God, these people formed a

Part VI: Conclusion

nation out of these epic journeys. The Israelites started the necessary institutions for a well-functioning society; the most prominent among them in the Promised Land was a new monotheistic religion.

Commandments (613) dictated to Moses by God structured Judaism (and Christianity). The Lord directed Moses in the formulation of rituals and ceremonies for this religion. Additionally, God gave instructions in these commandments for societal institutions, such as the judiciary, marriage, family, economy, and health.

What do we make of the sociology of religion? Believers may read this discipline as a denial of God and reject this way of thinking. Non-believers may seize upon the sociology of religion as an affirmation that God does not exist. But what does a sociologist of religion who is a Christian believe? Let us look at Peter Berger, who falls into this latter category:

> The contents of Christianity, like those of any other religious tradition, will have to be analyzed as human projections, and the [Christian theologian] will have to come to terms with the obvious discomforts caused thereby... Only after he has really grasped what it means to say that religion is a human product or projection can he begin to search, *within* this array of projections, for what may turn out to be signals of transcendance.[1]

Generations of people have read the first five books of the Bible, most notably Jews. Their belief in these words has held them together for millennia, through good times and bad. The Torah has created a resilient people. They have made extraordinary contributions to humankind in such fields as:

- Law (e.g., Ruth Bader Ginsburg),
- Philosophy (e.g., Spinoza),
- Science (e.g., Albert Einstein),
- Classical music (e.g., Gustav Mahler),
- Psychology (e.g., Sigmund Freud), and
- Literature (e.g., Franz Kafka).

1. Berger, *Sacred Canopy*. 184-185.

Finale

Some may read these Bible books and call them fables. One thing is for sure: they have given humanity souls who made our species a grander people.

Appendix A

Biblical Genealogy
From 4004 BCE to 30 AD

Appendix A

Figure A.1: Biblical genealogy from 4004 BCE to 30 AD

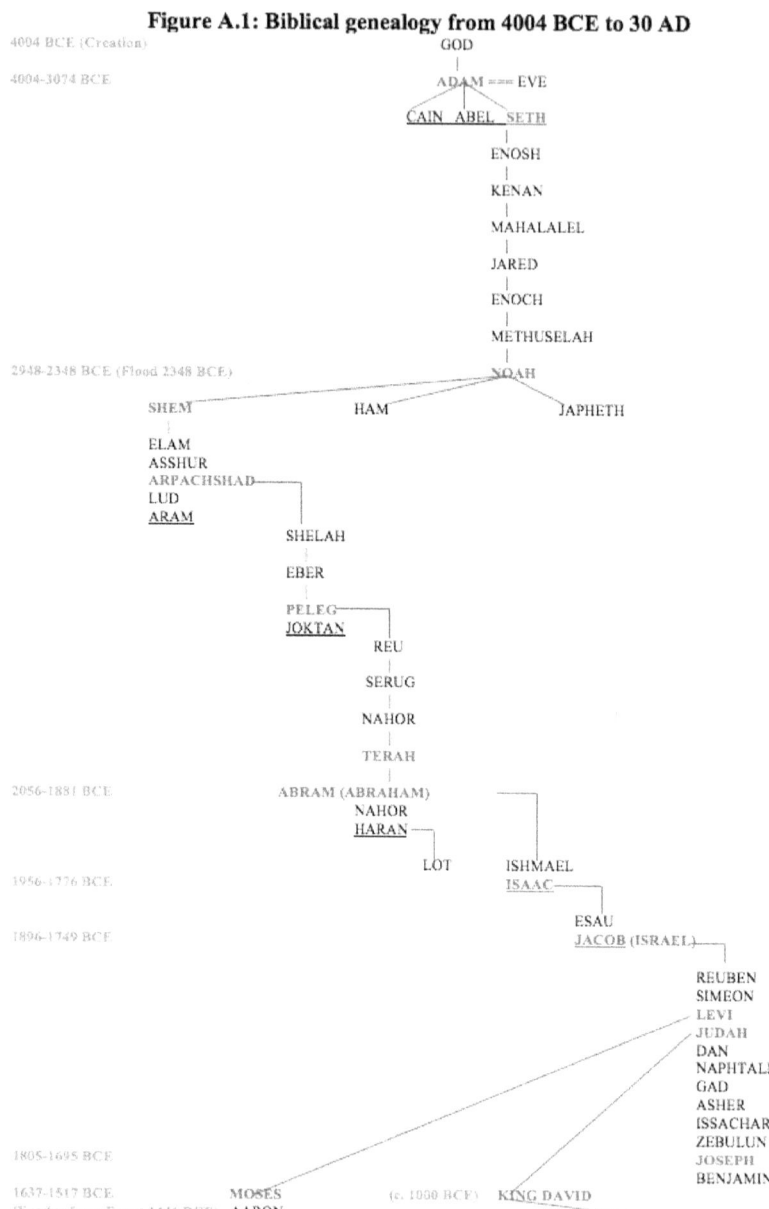

NOTE: Internet sites record different biblical dates.

Appendix B

World History in Biblical Times and Biblical Relationships

VIEWING THE PLAY AS described in chapter nine, an audience member may have had questions about the biblical story, perhaps like you. For instance, what was happening in world history at the time these holy people walked the earth? When did Noah live compared to, say, Abraham? Who was related to whom? That is, who was Noah's father? Appendix B answers these questions.

The biblical story in its first five books:

- *Genesis* covers the time between Adam and Joseph. It tells the story of Creation; humankind's life in and banishment from Paradise; Noah and the Great Flood; the first patriarchs of the Hebrews, Abraham; and Isaac, Jacob, and Joseph's life and times.

- *Exodus*, although known for the stories of Egyptian plagues, the Israelis' slavery, Moses' extraction of the Hebrews from Egypt, and the Ten Commandments, is filled with ordinances and laws concerning personal injuries; property rights; feasts and the Sabbath; ark and tabernacle construction; sanctuary offerings; and design of priests' garments. It ends with Israel's idol worship yielding to the replacement of the original Ten Commandments.

Appendix B

- A majority of *Leviticus* lists laws, rules, and regulations. Laws cover how to conduct offerings, such as burial, peace, and sin offerings. It records laws for eating the proper food; guidelines document how to test for leprosy and cleanse a leper's house. Laws cover immoral sexual relations and the famous "eye for an eye" dictum.

- The book of *Numbers* counts Israelite warriors and sets living standards for the camps that held them. Several religious directives are given, such as Aaron's benediction and rituals conducted during Passover. The Israelis complain about and rebel against their conditions in the desert, while Moses intercedes with God on their behalf. Before they conquer Canaan, Miriam and Aaron (Moses' sister and brother) die. A new cohort prepares to enter the Promised Land, replacing the generation of Israelis who left Egypt.

- *Deuteronomy* commences with a history of the chosen people from when they left Egypt to their wandering in the desert. The book lists rewards and punishment for people who obey and disobey God, respectively. Essentially, people gain a rich life in a secure land if they adhere to God's commandments, but they perish, as individuals and as a nation, if they disobey him. The book includes laws governing deviant behavior, such as physically harming another, maltreating captives of war, and falsely accusing one's wife of being deflowered. Deuteronomy (and the Torah/Pentateuch) ends with Moses' death and Joshua's selection as the leader of the Israelites. God charges him with taking his chosen into the Promised Land.

When we pay attention to the Bible, we narrow our perspective to biblical people, places, and events. However, one wonders if we draw back our awareness and look at the rest of the world, what we would see.

First, we start with people in the Bible and when they lived; then what was going on in the world during biblical times; and end with how people were related in the Bible.

World History in Biblical Times and Biblical Relationships

When Did Biblical Figures Live?

Figures B.1 list significant people, their ages (in parentheses), and the years they were alive in the first five books of the Bible. For instance, Moses lived 120 years from 1637 BCE to 1517 BCE.

Figure B.1: From Adam to Moses—Dates

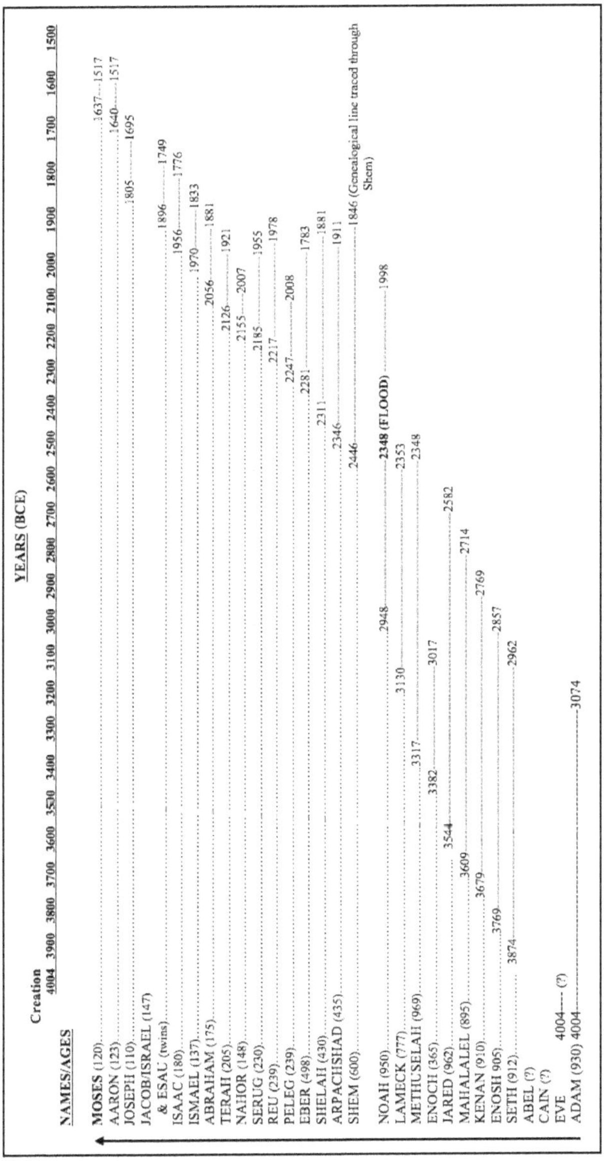

NAMES/AGES	YEARS (BCE)
MOSES (120)	1637–1517
AARON (123)	1640–1517
JOSEPH (110)	1805–1695
JACOB/ISRAEL (147) & ESAU (twins)	1896–1749
ISAAC (180)	1956–1776
ISMAEL (137)	1970–1833
ABRAHAM (175)	2056–1881
TERAH (205)	2126–1921
NAHOR (148)	2155–2007
SERUG (230)	2185–1955
REU (239)	2217–1978
PELEG (239)	2247–2008
EBER (498)	2281–1783
SHELAH (430)	2311–1881
ARPACHSHAD (435)	2346–1911
SHEM (600)	2446–1846 (Genealogical line traced through Shem)
	2348 (FLOOD)
NOAH (950)	2948–1998
	2353
LAMECK (777)	3130–2353
METHUSELAH (969)	3317–2348
ENOCH (365)	3382–3017
JARED (962)	3544–2582
MAHALALEL (895)	3609–2714
KENAN (910)	3679–2769
ENOSH (905)	3769–2857
SETH (912)	3874–2962
ABEL (?)	
CAIN (?)	
EVE	4004–(?)
ADAM (930)	4004–3074

Creation: 4004

Appendix B

As Figure B.1 shows, the first five books of the Bible cover the time between Adam's birth (4004 BCE) and Moses' death (1517 BCE). Between Adam's creation (4004 BCE) and Noah's survival of the Great Flood (2348 BCE), 1,656 years passed. From Noah's time to Moses' death (1517 BCE), 831 years passed. All together the first five books of the Bible cover approximately 2,500 years of history (4004 BCE to 1517 BCE). Quite an epic.

What Was Going On in the Rest of the World as This Narrative Played Out?

Historians note the Stone, Bronze, and Iron Ages as early epochs in human development. They got their names from the predominant technology humans employed during these periods. During the Stone Age (2.5 million years ago to 3300 BCE), humans lived in small groups that moved around to hunt animals and gather plants.. They used stones for tools and weapons. During the Bronze Age (3300 BCE to 1200 BCE), humans learned to mix copper with tin to form bronze. They made tools, weapons, and household goods, among other items, from this metal alloy. Bronze Age nomads settled into city-states, and these people built massive edifices, including temples. In the Iron Age (1200 BCE to 600 BCE), people fashioned iron and steel to make tools and weapons. During this time, many Bronze Age civilizations in Mesopotamia and the Middle East collapsed while major cultures developed in Greece, Italy, and Persia.

Methuselah's lifetime (3317 to 2348 BCE) saw the development of farming, city-states, and grand buildings. However, those living in Europe, North and South America, and Southeast Asia were still hunters and gatherers. In other words, some places where human development bloomed were the same locations where biblical figures lived.

Many hold biblical events as retold myths from earlier civilizations. The Great Flood story is strangely similar to a flood covered in the Sumerian Epic of Gilgamesh written over 2,600 years

World History in Biblical Times and Biblical Relationships

before Noah. In this tale, Utnapishtim built a circular-shaped boat that carried relatives and animals that endured days of storms.[1]

So, events in the first five books of the Bible happened during the Bronze Age when Middle Eastern, Egyptian, and some people in the Indian and Chinese cultures were developing their civilizations. Less developed people populated Europe, the Americas, and Oceania.

How Were People in the Bible Related?

Figure B.2 establishes family lines recorded in Genesis from Adam and Eve to Noah's sons, Shem, Ham, and Japheth.

Figure B.2: Genesis 4 and 5 Genealogy—Adam and Eve to Shem

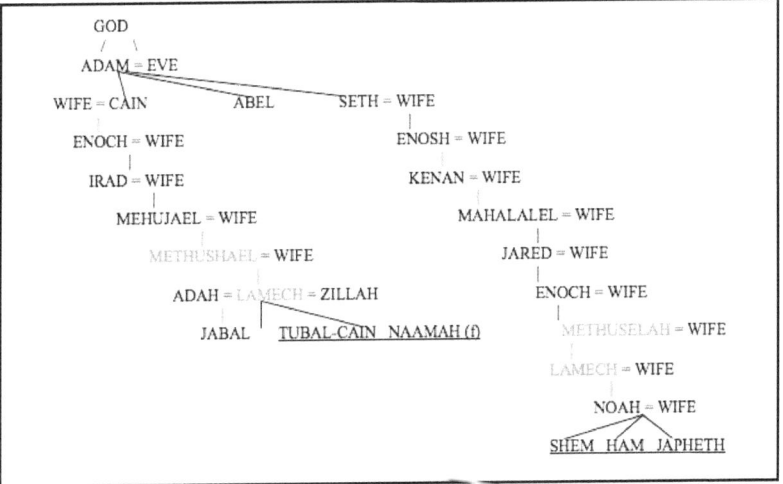

God created Adam (Gen 2:7) out of the dust and Eve (Gen 2:21–22) from Adam's rib. Adam and Eve were husband and wife. As Earth's first parents, they produced three children: Cain (Gen 4:1), Abel (Gen 4:2), and Seth (Gen 4:25), among others. Cain killed Abel, and consequently, God banished him and his descendants

---

1. Tharoor, "Before Noah."

Appendix B

from Eden. When he was in the Land of Nod, Cain had relations with his wife (unnamed), who gave birth to Enoch (Gen 4:17). Abel was physically dead, and Cain was spiritually deceased because he killed his brother. Abel and Cain's absences left Seth to carry the family line, which led to Jesus.

Methuselah lived in the seventh generation after Adam and Eve. He was notable on two accounts. First, he was the oldest person in the Bible. He lived for 696 years. Second, Methuselah was 187 years old when he sired Lamech (Gen 5:25). Lamech was 182 years old when he had Noah (Gen 5:29). Noah was 500 years old when he had Shem, Ham, and Japheth (Gen 5:32).[2] So, Noah's grandfather was Methuselah.

Not until Genesis 9 is the biblical genealogy picked up again.[3] Only Ham's son, Canaan, is mentioned in Gen 9:18, but Genesis 10 cites Noah's other descendants.

Figure B.3 and B.3.1 present Noah's descendants. The author of Genesis scatters these people throughout eighteen chapters, between chapter 10 and chapter 50.

---

[2]. Confusion arises in Genesis 4–5. Genesis 4:18 cites Methushael as Lamech's father. In Genesis 5:25, however, Methuselah fathers Lamech. Are Methushael and Methuselah one or two people? Likewise, is Lamech in Genesis 4 the same person in Genesis 5? In other words, are we looking at one or two genealogical lines? Advocates argue both sides. Many argue, however, that Jesus' line followed through Seth. If so, this indicates two family lines.

[3]. Genesis 5 and 9 describe the Great Flood.

World History in Biblical Times and Biblical Relationships

Figure B.3: Genesis 10–11, 16, 19, 21–22, 24–25, 28–30, 34–35 Genealogy—Noah's descendants

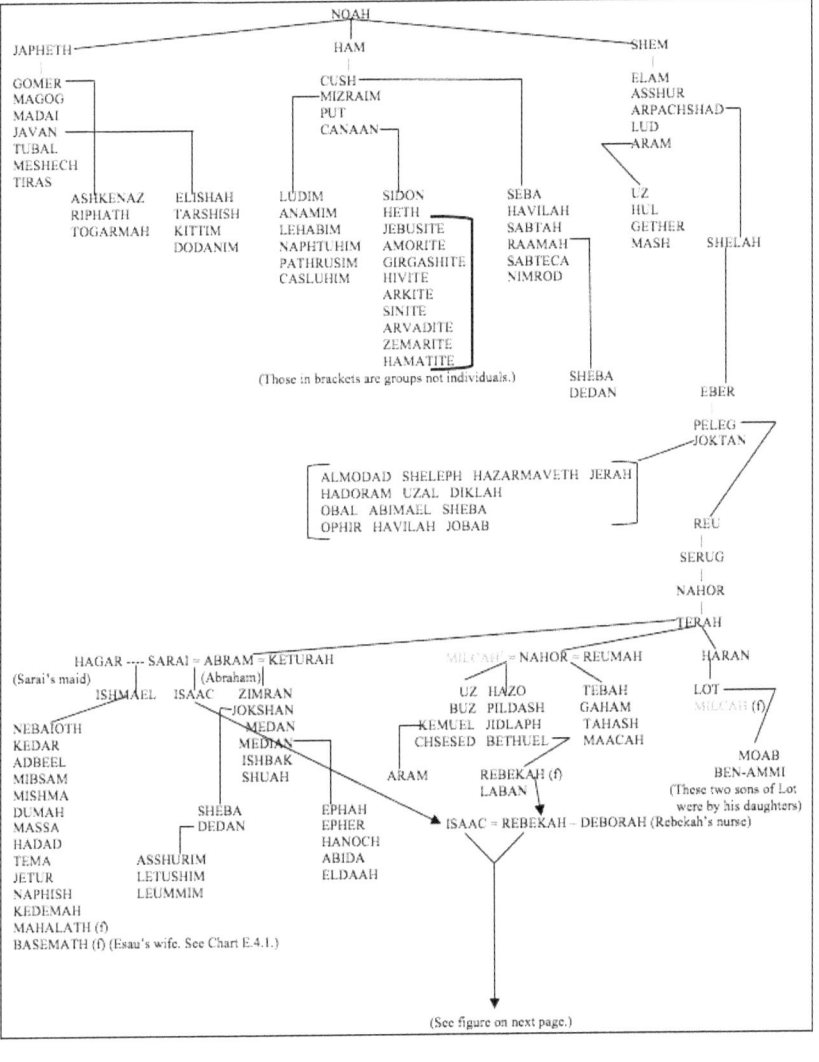

Appendix B

Figure B.3.1: Genesis 35–36, 38, 41, 46, and 50 genealogy—Noah's descendants
(Figure B.3.1 is a continuation of Figure B.3.)

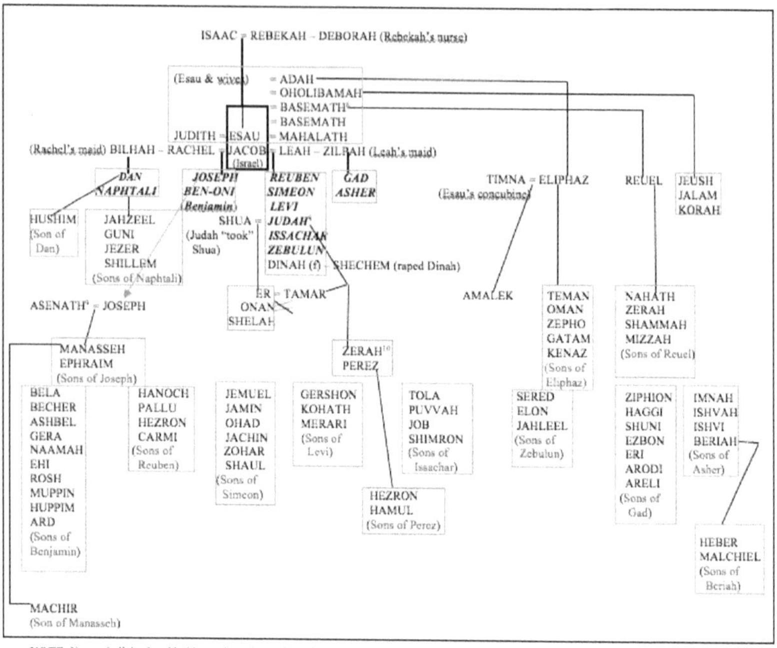

[Genealogy chart showing descendants of Isaac and Rebekah, including Esau's and Jacob's lines, with the twelve tribes of Israel indicated. Key figures include:
- ISAAC = REBEKAH – DEBORAH (Rebekah's nurse)
- Esau & wives: ADAH, OHOLIBAMAH, BASEMATH, BASEMATH, MAHALATH, JUDITH
- ESAU = JACOB (Israel)
- Jacob's wives: BILHAH (Rachel's maid), RACHEL, LEAH, ZILPAH (Leah's maid)
- Sons: DAN, NAPHTALI, JOSEPH, BEN-ONI (Benjamin), REUBEN, SIMEON, LEVI, JUDAH (Judah "took" Shua), ISSACHAR, ZEBULUN, DINAH (f), GAD, ASHER
- TIMNA = ELIPHAZ (Esau's concubine), REUEL, JEUSH, JALAM, KORAH
- HUSHIM (Son of Dan)
- JAHZEEL, GUNI, JEZER, SHILLEM (Sons of Naphtali)
- ER = TAMAR, ONAN, SHELAH; ZERAH, PEREZ
- SHECHEM (raped Dinah), AMALEK
- TEMAN, OMAN, ZEPHO, GATAM, KENAZ (Sons of Eliphaz)
- NAHATH, ZERAH, SHAMMAH, MIZZAH (Sons of Reuel)
- ASENATH = JOSEPH; MANASSEH, EPHRAIM (Sons of Joseph)
- BELA, BECHER, ASHBEL, GERA, NAAMAH, EHI, ROSH, MUPPIM, HUPPIM, ARD (Sons of Benjamin)
- HANOCH, PALLU, HEZRON, CARMI (Sons of Reuben)
- JEMUEL, JAMIN, OHAD, JACHIN, ZOHAR, SHAUL (Sons of Simeon)
- GERSHON, KOHATH, MERARI (Sons of Levi)
- HEZRON, HAMUL (Sons of Perez)
- TOLA, PUVVAH, JOB, SHIMRON (Sons of Issachar)
- SERED, ELON, JAHLEEL (Sons of Zebulun)
- ZIPHION, HAGGI, SHUNI, EZBON, ERI, ARODI, ARELI (Sons of Gad)
- IMNAH, ISHVAH, ISHVI, BERIAH (Sons of Asher)
- HEBER, MALCHIEL (Sons of Beriah)
- MACHIR (Son of Manasseh)]

NOTE: Names italicized and bold constitute the twelve tribes of Israel.

Nine generations after Noah, Terah was born, and he fathered Abraham (as well as Nahor and Haran). Abraham fathered Isaac (along with other children). Isaac's wife (Rebekah) gave birth to Jacob (among other children), who had twelve sons who founded the twelve tribes of Israel. Abraham, Isaac, and Jacob are considered patriarchs of the Hebrew people. How were these patriarchs related?

Terah produced three sons: Abram (Abraham), Nahor, and Haran. So, Abraham, Nahor, and Haran were brothers. Haran fathered Lot, who was Abraham's nephew.

Abraham was the Israelites' first patriarch. He was the first to lead God's chosen people out of Mesopotamia to the Promised Land.[4] Abraham had two wives in his lifetime: Sarai (Sarah) and

---

4. Later, in Exodus, Moses leads the Israelites out of Egypt to the Promised Land.

World History in Biblical Times and Biblical Relationships

Keturah. Also, he bedded Sarah's maid, Hagar. Abraham and Hagar had Ismael while Abraham sired six children with Keturah.[5] Abraham's most famous offspring, however, was Isaac, whose mother was Sarah. Ishmael and Isaac were half-brothers, having the same father, Abraham, but different mothers—Ishmael's mother was Hagar; Isaac's mother was Sarah.

Isaac, the second patriarch, married Rebekah. They had two sons, Esau and Jacob. Isaac wanted to bless Esau but Rebekah wanted him to bless Jacob. She told Jacob to feign Esau's identity. The deception worked.: Isaac blessed Jacob instead of Esau. Since his father recognized Jacob, he became the Israelites' third patriarch. Note that Abraham's son was Isaac, and Jacob was his grandson (see Figure B.4).

Figure B.4: Abraham's sons and grandsons

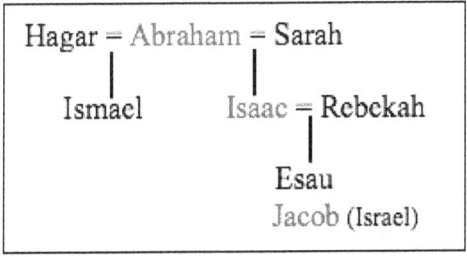

God changed Jacob's name to Israel; his wives were Leah and Rachel. Also, he bedded Leah's maid, Zilpah, as well as Rachel's maid, Bilhah. He fathered twelve sons who became the heads of the twelve tribes of Israel: Reuben, Simeon, Levi, Judah, Issachar, Zebulun, Joseph, Benjamin, Dan, Naphtali, Gad, and Asher. The following were full brothers: Dan and Naphtali (their mother was Bilhah, Rachel's maid); Joseph and Benjamin (their mother was Rachel); Reuben, Simeon, Levi, Judah, Issachar, and Zebulun (their mother was Leah; Dinah was their full sister); Gad and Asher (their mother was Zilpah, Leah's maid).

---

5. Abraham and Keturah had these children: Zimran, Jokshan, Medan, Median, Ishbak, and Shuah.

Appendix B

Consequently, many of these men were half-brothers. Thus, the twelve tribes of Israel were offspring of their father, Jacob (Israel); grandsons of Isaac; and Abraham's great-grandsons. Half-brothers Joseph and Levi played significant roles later in the biblical narrative. Joseph led the chosen people to Egypt and prospered before their enslavement. Levi produced priests for God.

Finally, two famous individuals recognized by many Bible readers are Lot and Onan. Who were they, and how were they related?

Lot's father was Haran, who was Abraham's brother, so Lot was Abraham's nephew. Lot holds the infamous position of fathering his daughters' children. Unbeknownst to Lot, his daughters seduced him. Why? They feared remaining single since they lived in a remote area after God led their family out of the destroyed city of Sodom.

Onan's mother and father were Shua and Judah (a son of Jacob and Leah). Onan's brothers were Er and Shelah. Er was married to Tamar, but God killed Er because he was evil. Since Judah's daughter-in-law was a widow, he promised her Onan. Onan refused to marry Tamar because he knew the community would not recognize their offspring, so he spilled his seed on the ground.

Ishmael and Lot were, respectively, son and nephew of the Israeli's first patriarch, Abraham. Onan, on the other hand, was a grandson of the third patriarch, Jacob. More than 100 years separated Ishmael and Lot from Onan.

Finally, within Genesis, there are approximately 425 named family relatives—quite a cast of characters. Additionally, we unearth at least fifteen groups, such as Canaanites, Moabites, and Hittites. Genesis contains more characters than a Russian novel!

Bibliography

Books

Berger, Peter L. *The Sacred Canopy: Elements of a Sociological Theory of Religion*. New York: Anchor Books, 1969.

———. "Sociology as a Form of Consciousness." in *Tales from Wildwood: A Sociology for HACC*. Edited by Robert Deitzel, et al., 3–12. Xerox College, 1973.

Broom, Leonard, and Philip Selznick. *Sociology: A Text with Adapted Readings*. 3rd ed. New York: Harper & Row, 1963.

Classic Comparative Parallel Bible (*New American Standard Bible Version*, 1995). Grand Rapids: Zondervan, 2011.

Dressler, David. *Sociology: The Study of Human Interaction*. New York: Alfred A. Knopf, 1969.

Goffman, Erving. *The Presentation of Self in Everyday Life*. New York: Doubleday, 1959.

Heapes, John R. *Other Worlds: UFOs, Aliens, and the Afterlife*. Bloomington: iUniverse, 2014.

Macionis, John J. *Society: The Basics*. 11th ed. New York: Pearson, 2011.

Parrillo, Vincent N. *Stranger to These Shores: Race and Ethnic Relations in the United States*. 4th ed. Hoboken: Prentice Hall, 1993.

Schenck, Ferdinand S. *Sociology of the Bible*. New York: Board of Publication of the Reformed Church of America, 1909.

Shakespeare, William. *As You Like It*. Act 2, Scene 7.

Webpages

Ancient Code team. "Before Noah's Great Flood: Here are 3 Flood Stories That Predate The Bible." Ancient Code. 2021. https://.ancient-code.com/before-noahs-great-flood-here-are-3-flood-stories-that-predate-the-bible/.

Aron. "Differences Between Rituals and Ceremonies." DifferenceBetween.com. July 11, 2011. https://www.differencebetween.com/difference-between-rituals-and-vs-ceremonies/.

Bibliography

Bible History. "The Holy Materials." Bible History Online. https://www.bible-history.com/tabernacle/tab4preparing_for_the_tabernacle.htm.

Bible Info. "Who wrote the Bible?" BibleInfo.com. bibleinfo.com/en/questions/who-wrote-the-bible.

Cambridge University Press. "Bibles." Cambridge University Press. 2021. http://www.cambridge.org/bibles/bible-versions/#sffe5s3VjwFyGuy9.97.

Enns, Pete. "Gilgamesh, Atrahasis and the Flood." BioLogos. June 1, 2010. https://biologoss.org/articles/gilgamesh-atrahasis-and-the-flood/.

Garrett, Jeremiah K. "The 5 Offerings in the Old Testament." Seedbed. July 29, 2014. https://www.seedbed.com/5-offerings-old-testament/.

Hodge, Bodie, and Terry Mortenson. "Did Moses Write Genesis?" Answers in Genesis. June 2, 2011. https://answeringgenesis.org/bible-characters/moses/did-moses-write-genesis/.

The Interactive Bible. "Why Are There Different Versions of the Bible?" The Interactive Bible. March 2020. http://www.bible.ca/b-many-versions.html.

Jewish Virtual Library. "Judaism: The Written Law - Torah." Jewish Virtual Library. 2021. https://www.jewishvirtuallibrary.org/the-written-law-torah.

Kranz, Jeffrey. "The 35 Authors Who Wrote the Bible [Chart + Illustrations]." Overview Bible. August 9, 2018. https://overviewbible.com/authors-who-wrote-bible/.

Linker, Reba. "Wandering in the Desert." The Huffington Post. December 6, 2017. https://www.huffpost.com/entry/wandering-in-the-desert_b_9759052#:~:text=The%20distance%20from%20Egypt%20to,the%20desert%20for%20forty%20years.

Macky, Ian. PAT. November 28, 2018. https://ian.macky.net/pat/.

McQueen, Mark, and Martha McQueen. "Mt. Sinai, Kadesh Barnea, and the Exodus." Dawn to Dusk. October 11, 2012. http://www.dawntoduskpublications.com/html/BT/12/Kadesh-Barnea-Route-Exodus-short.htm.

New World Encyclopedia contributors. "Vedic Period." New World Encyclopedia. May 7, 2020. https://www.newworldencyclopedia.org/entry/Vedic_Period.

Orr, James. "Deuteronomy." International Standard Bible Encyclopedia. 1915. https://www.biblestudytools.com/dictionary/deuteronomy/.

———. "Sinai." International Standard Bible Encyclopedia. 1915. https://www.biblestudytools.com/dictionary/sinai/.

Rudd, Steven. "The Exodus Route: Travel times, distances, rates of travel, days of week." The Interactive Bible. May 2020. http://www.bible.ca/archeology/bible-archeology-exodus-route-travel-times-distances-days.htm.

Reference.com Staff Writer. "How Many Copies of the Bible Have Been Sold?" Reference.com. March 29, 2020. reference.com/world-view/many-copies-bible-sold.

Schechter, Sara. "Deuteronomy." The Israel Bible. 2021. https://theisraelbible.com/bible/deuteronomy.

Schulman, Marc. "Hadrian's Wall." Multieducator. 1996–2020. https://www.historycentral.com/dates/100ad.html.

Bibliography

Tharoor, Ishaan. "Before Noah: Myths of the Flood Are Far Older Than the Bible." Time. April 1, 2014. https://time.com/44631/noah-christians-flood-aronofsky/#:~:text=The%20story%20of%20Noah%20may%20be%20part%20of.origins%2C%20rooted%20in%20the%20ancient%civilizations%20of%20Mesopotamia.

Valkanet, Rich. "Bible Timeline." Bible Hub. 2020.https://biblehub.com/timeline/

Wallace, Daniel B. "Choosing a Bible Translation." Crosswalk. Com. 3 May, 2010. https://www.crosswalk.com/faith/spiritual-life/choosing-a-bible-translation-11631126.html

Ward, Mark. "5 Guidelines for Picking the Right Bible Translation." Logos. 25 May, 2016. https://blog.logos.com/2016/05/5-guidelines-for-picking-the-right-bible-translation-for-the-right-situation/

Wallace, Daniel B. "Choosing a Bible Translation." Crosswalk.com. 3 May, 2010. https://www.crosswalk.com/faith/spiritual-life/choosing-a-bible-translation-11631126.html.

Ward, Mark. "% Guidelines for Picking the Right Bible Translation." Logos. 25 May, 2016. https://blog.logos.com/2016/05/5-guidelines-for-picking-the-right-translation-for-the-right-situation/.

www.ingramcontent.com/pod-product-compliance
Lightning Source LLC
Chambersburg PA
CBHW051926160426
43198CB00012B/2056